Praise for *Towards Culturally Appropriate Behaviour Support*

Linda and her family have lived on, and visited Mununjali land near Mount Barney, MacPherson Ranges, for over a century. As members of the Mununjali people, we appreciate the ongoing support and connection that she has brought to our community.

I collaborated with Patricia O'Connor, a proud Mununjali descendant, and together we saw the merits of this respectful and extremely relevant tool (document) to be used by educators within the Indigenous System. As an Aboriginal Education Officer with the Commonwealth Government ABSEC in the early 1980s, I travelled Western Queensland and saw, and realised back then, the void and the need for such a brilliant school-based tool. Indigenous students require many and varied methods of communication that are specific to culture and environment which are not always seen in mainstream classrooms.

It is our great pleasure to endorse this groundbreaking and exciting contribution to the much-needed education framework for our Indigenous children across Australia.

Matthew O'Connor, Dip Ed(Sec) QLD
President of KACC and The Yugambeh Museum

Kombumerri Elder Patricia O'Connor, co-founder of Kombumerri Aboriginal Corporation for Culture (KACC) T/A The 'Yugambeh Museum', enjoys the engagement with Linda's work and follows closely its development. Patricia wishes Linda every success with its launching and its acceptance by the teaching community.

Patricia O'Connor, BA (Anthropology) QLD

Towards Culturally Appropriate Behaviour Support provides an opportunity for individuals, schools and communities alike to contemplate how their interwoven working relationships impact the behaviours of the students within our classrooms. Dr Linda Llewellyn examines these uncomplicated yet fundamental concepts through sharing the rich lived experiences of Indigenous Australians and provides specific examples of what teachers can do in each instance. This book offers insights for educators to look with curiosity at their own capabilities in this space. An easy read with practical tools for classrooms.

Dr Caroline Blackley, Director of Blackley Group Pty Ltd,
Founder of Four Dimensions and the 4D Framework

Towards Culturally Appropriate Behaviour Support is an easy-to-read guide for educators working with Aboriginal and Torres Strait Islander children and families. The practical information for day-to-day implementation is supplemented with eye-opening anecdotes from Indigenous students, educators and family members. A must-read for both the experienced and those who are new to the field.

Tania Fragnito BEd(Prim), BECE, MEd and Theol

Linda provides us with a comprehensive introduction for those new to First Nations teaching and a gentle reminder and reliable lenses for experienced teacher reflection. This book models privileging of Indigenous 'fields and habitus', culture habits, strengths and knowledge – Indigenous perspectives – demanding the empathy and accountability of the teacher. It's a necessary read.

Veronica Graham BSc, MEd, PhD, Science Teacher

Towards Culturally Appropriate Behaviour Support

Towards Culturally Appropriate Behaviour Support

Teacher attitudes and strategies to support
Australian Indigenous students

Dr Linda Llewellyn

amba
press

Published in 2025 by Amba Press, Melbourne, Australia
www.ambapress.com.au

Cover design: Tess McCabe
Cover artwork: Natalie Jade
Internal design: Amba Press
Editor: Rica Dearman

ISBN: 9781923215344 (pbk)
ISBN: 9781923215351 (ebk)

A catalogue record for this book is available from the National Library of Australia.

Contents

Author's note

Please note that, unlike the thesis, some words have been removed from interview participants' statements for fluency, for example, 'um', 'you know' and duplications that did not add meaning.

Foreword

It is an absolute privilege to be penning this foreword. I first crossed paths with Linda during the early 2000s, as a student, completing my Bachelor of Education. Unlike my other teachers, and perhaps owing to guidance from afar, Linda and I have maintained contact. I say that because, I too, put emphasis on relational-based teaching as a cornerstone of success for Indigenous students.

I completed my bachelor's degree through the Remote Area Teacher Education Program, the focus of the course being Indigenous perspectives of education, at the primary school level. The patent advantage, and major attraction to me, was the mode of delivery. I was able to apply theory, and appreciate its impacts, in my context, my home community of Kubin.

In this setting, I was fortunate to utilise the expertise of the Elders in the community. By including the Elders, I was creating an appreciation of being a part of a whole, that has been honed by the rest of time. They taught me the immense value of the unsaid – support with the spoken instruction and the appropriateness of gestures and body language.

As was the case with my own journey to become a registered teacher, this book respects, incorporates and mimics the teaching behaviours of our authentic Indigenous *mat**. It acknowledges that we are all lifelong learners. The Indigenous perspectives, via the authentic voice inserts, are similar to my Elders' teaching of the mat that furnished the fireplace in times past.

---

*   *Mat* is both a place and a way. Reflecting at a day's end while restoking for the tomorrow. There would be no other light, so was born the importance of time and place. The Elders would be leading the reflection and yarning of anecdotes.

I know that when this book is read as a learner, you will engage, thereby making you a better teacher – through trial and error. It will equip your toolbox with much more than mere tools but means of enriching lives; your own and that of your students. This will have generational reverberating effects. Using a metaphor, I would see this book as a map through our intricate and precious reefs, to flow in the calm waters of electrical thunderstorms.

I hope you all find what you need, and all the very best in your respective professional journeys.

Wa wa...

Kaltie W Tabuai, BEd (Indigenous)
Elder
Kubin Community

Introduction

Student behaviour causes stress and sleepless nights for teachers. It is the third most common reason for new graduates leaving the profession within their first five years. Within that global concern, Indigenous students face disproportionate levels of suspensions and exclusion. There is a problem with the preparedness of teachers to support the behaviour of all students, but particularly for Indigenous students (First Nations has become a popular term, but I will use the language that was used by my Indigenous participants at the time of the interviews).

I had been successful with the most difficult classes and students in mainstream schools, including having great experiences with the Indigenous students in those classes. Before I left the state system, I worked as a behaviour support teacher across six high schools. After 20 years or so of teaching experience, when I first went to a 100% Indigenous school to teach, I was not prepared for the cultural differences. My learning curve was steep, and I am grateful to the Indigenous teacher aides and liaison officers who helped me learn. I became an assistant principal in secondary in that school. I worked as an education officer for Catholic education and increased my skill set. My PhD thesis enabled me to investigate the differences in behaviour support for Indigenous students, making a conscious decision on how to succeed with them.

As mentioned, Indigenous students are disproportionately receiving suspensions and exclusions in schools. Research has shown that systems and schools create inequitable situations for Indigenous students. My work focused on teacher actions in their classrooms. Some teachers get along with Indigenous students and some do not. Students will work and cooperate for some teachers and not for others.

In the words of one liaison officer, *"I've definitely noticed children acting one way for one teacher and another way for another, especially even between the teacher to school officer as well. Even with me, they might refuse to do their work in the classroom for the teacher and then I will take them away and they'll slowly but surely get the job done... That, though, whether it be because they are Indigenous or just because they are getting that constant hounding, you know, getting actually away and having that time just with them?"*

Just last week I was explaining the topic of my research to a university student who related that when she was at school, a teacher blamed a visibly Indigenous boy and the class collectively backed him against the teacher. She is not visibly Indigenous and was irate at the unconscious bias of the teacher. Teachers can examine their attitudes and biases and learn strategies to create successful relationships with their Indigenous students.

Before we start

I would like to acknowledge the Traditional Owners of the areas where I work and where the study was conducted. I would also like to thank the Indigenous staff, students, families and friends who participated in the study or advised me throughout. The results of the first phase of my PhD are included in this book, from interviews with Indigenous staff, students and family members. The second phase took those suggestions, refined them into a survey instrument and took the first step to finding validity for them. The third phase took the suggestions into the classroom as an observation tool, exploring the relationship between teacher use of the suggestions and student on task time and student satisfaction after engaging with the teacher. The results are available in my thesis and are mentioned briefly before the conclusion of this book.

There are two distinct cultures in Australia's Indigenous peoples, and within those, many separate cultures, with their own languages and customs. Non-Indigenous Australians should be aware and respectful of those cultures. Within those cultures, families may also be different. Therefore, my recommendations in this book must be considered within the knowledge that they are context specific. Local peoples must be considered when you implement the strategies.

Many researchers have suggested ways to create environments that are culturally relevant for teaching and are welcoming. Australian studies have suggested improvements through examining culturally responsive pedagogy (Lewthwaite et al., 2015), listening, using a Reggio Emilia style (Morrison et al., 2019) and pedagogical changes (Burgess et al., 2022; Lowe et al., 2021; Yunkaporta, 2009; Yunkaporta & Kirby, 2011). One suggestion from a friend was to use Indigenous methodologies such as yarning circles. My work sits alongside those, to prepare teachers for times when behaviour support may be necessary. Some systems should change to accommodate their habitus and cultural capital. I am not implying that Indigenous students have deficits, or that Indigenous students do not succeed – Indigenous students *do* excel. My topic and advice are based on where I work, and this study has grown out of that context.

After reading widely, I was able to summarise the information in literature in a set of themes. These themes were a way to group and condense the suggestions that came from the Indigenous interview participants, and present them to teachers in a way that they could remember and apply them. I made a distinction between strategies which can be implemented without much thought and attitudes which require some reflection and possibly internal change for teachers. I have called these attitudes and strategies, suggested by my Indigenous participants, the TASSAIS Themes: Teacher Attitudes and Strategies to Support Australian Indigenous Students. There are three outside themes in the graphic over the page that are the larger picture. The themes are:

1. Knowledge of self and other in the socio, historical, political context.
2. Knowledge of students and their cultures without a deficit notion of difference (bias).
3. Connections with families and communities.

The themes related to teacher qualities are inside the bigger picture ovals:

4. Teacher qualities.
5. Positive relationships (which sits inside teacher qualities. It was important in the literature and interviews and required special attention).

The attitudes and strategies that can be implemented are sorted into:

6. Pedagogies that support behaviour.
7. Proactive behaviour support strategies.
8. Reactive behaviour support strategies.

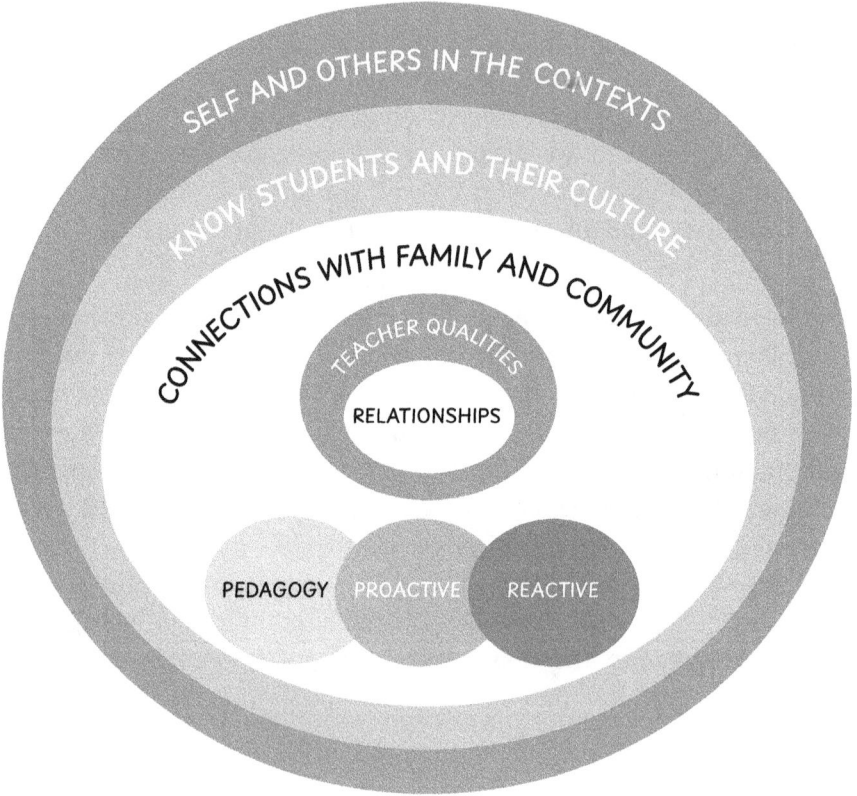

The TASSAIS Themes

The TASSAIS attitudes and strategies survey is available online (Llewellyn, 2023; TASSAIS Survey, 2023). You may like to try a baseline data collection for your personal growth. If you design a unique login, you can measure the frequency of use of the attitudes and strategies before and after increasing your awareness (self-reported). Online or face-to-face training – which will go into further depth – is available from

Llewellyn Consultancy; find out more at llewellyn-consultancy.com. You can repeat the survey when you feel you have internalised and implemented some of the TASSAIS attitudes and strategies. I can evaluate a video segment using direct observation data when you are ready, so you can see your improvement.

Initial suggestions put forward by Indigenous participants have been processed through the workshop, focus group Rasch analysis (Bond et al., 2020) as well as classroom observations. You can find details of this process in my thesis. Each chapter in this book covers a theme, relates to suggestions from Indigenous participants and proposes how teachers can implement them. At the end of each chapter, the evidence-supported TASSAIS items are presented.

You could also ask for mentoring from an Indigenous person in your local area as your context may differ. You can implement strategies in your teaching, while attitudes require some internal change for teachers. In the lists at the end of each theme, the attitudes and strategies are listed. Take some time to reflect on these. In order to be authentic and avoid misunderstanding, the words of the Indigenous participants are included, rather than my interpretation of their intent.

You'll find further training and observation on my Teachable site: llewellyn-consultancy.teachable.com.

All participants interviewed were Aboriginal and/or Torres Strait Islander (Indigenous).

Theme 1:
Knowledge of self and other in the socio, historical, political context

"Indigenous student 'misbehaviour' is generally misinterpreted in isolation as both students and teachers arrive at school with differing perspectives secured from their life experiences outside the classroom."

(Gillan, 2008, p. 58)

Teachers need to understand the history and social and political landscape in which they work. This includes an awareness of power relationships, the effects of unconscious bias and a deficit notion of difference. I had been working with Indigenous students for about 15 years and caught myself in a moment of unconscious bias. A grandmother had come to the boarding school where I worked from the community and was sniffing and walking around the staffroom, obviously looking for tissues. I carried travel packs of tissues and offered her a pack. She took the pack and turned away without saying anything. I was momentarily stunned by her response. In my culture, one would say "thank you", take one tissue and return the pack. Halfway through that thought I mentally smacked myself over the head and reminded myself that, in her culture, her response was appropriate. She was complimenting me by accepting my offer, no thanks were necessary in her culture, and she needed the whole pack.

Teachers may not even be aware of their own culture; they may be like fish swimming in water, not aware that the water is there! The colour-blindness (treating all students the same) described in current literature and evident in local practices is often seen as the right thing to do. This misses cultural nuances that can be examined using Bourdieuian theory (Houston, 2002). Essentially, we understand, a school is a cultural field that replicates the dominant culture. If teachers are not aware that education is biased towards the dominant culture, they may not understand that some students lack cultural capital (unconscious skills found in the 'hidden curriculum' of schools) in this field; and in turn, judge them for lacking such cultural capital. In some classrooms, children learn that 'being' who they are is not valued and understood by those authorised to shape their learning conditions – teachers. They are, in other words, learning the aspects of their identity, leading to particular kinds of responses from teachers, which may positively or negatively impact upon them.

It is not just the colour of skin or cultural background that helps teachers to recognise students who are like themselves and students who are not. Markers of habitus include ways of being and speaking in an environment. If teachers are not aware of their own culture and habitus, they will interpret behaviour through their own habitus and can misinterpret student behaviour. This mismatch of habitus can also be viewed as part of the 'hidden curriculum' that functions in schools. This will impact students who come to school without relevant habitus, and cultural capital. They may suffer from teachers misunderstanding their behaviour. If we, as teachers, are unaware of our own culture, and unaware of the context, unconscious bias is likely to happen. In my graphic of the TASSAIS Themes on page 6, this theme fits into the bigger picture surrounding our work.

Why examine who you are in the context?

What Indigenous participants said

Participants in my study suggested that teachers get to know harmful impacts of colonisation on our Aboriginal and Torres Strait Islander cultures. One liaison officer relayed her history: *"For some reason, people seem to think it happened so long ago, and they always say, 'Oh! Get over it, move on.' I give it [gave] up my last job; one of the managers who was Indigenous, she was saying, 'It's time to move on and forget about the L-O-R-E and bring in the L-A-W, like that L-O-R-E that's the past and that's gone.' And I'm like, 'No, that's in here, that's with us all the way.' And she's like, 'No.' I'm thinking, 'Oh, my God, you're obviously very mainstream...' It's hard, 'cause my family was from [an island]. You don't see any Indigenous people on there anymore. It's just all tourists, and when I went there, I stayed in the [island's] hotel. They had a tour thing that I went on. And in the whole tour, they didn't talk one thing about Indigenous people, it's just like, 'This is the island; this is here, and this is there.' And I'm thinking, they don't talk anything about it probably because the history is so gruesome, you know, they just massacred so many of them. Like thousands of them, pushed them out to sea and let them drown. As I said, I have a great-uncle; he was old when he told the story... I say, you can't tell anybody to get rid of that side and only go for the L-A-W 'cause this is strong in a lot of people."*

Her great-uncle and his sister hid in a tree trunk as children and were the only surviving members of their people. For this staff member, historical tragedies caused by acts of colonisation are both real and recent. In a town near her, *"They used to sit in the back of utes and chase them at nighttime with their big shining lights and have guns, and whoever can shoot the most Aboriginal people was like the winner or something. It's all a big game to them... 'Cause for me, 'cause I am not dark, I am fair-skinned, I can go to parties all the time and my friends would say [they have] the same skin colour as me. They'll go, 'Do you ever get when you go to parties that happens a lot where people sit down, all of a sudden, they'll break into about Aboriginal people. And they talk about how all they do is sit around [at] parties and drink and blah. And they just bag them out in front of you. You, you're just sitting there around and having a few drinks or something, the conversations happen all the time.' And I just listen and listen and listen to everything they say and then I go, 'Oh, OK, well, I'm sorry you feel that way about Indigenous people, because I actually happen to be Aboriginal myself. My father is an Aboriginal man.' And then they go, 'Oh, my God, I'm so sorry, blah blah.' And I [say], 'You don't have to be sorry. Obviously, that's how you feel, but let me explain my culture to you.' And then I explain things to them and they go, 'Oh, OK, I didn't know that.' Like, I never get aggressive and swear [at] them or whatever, I'll just think in my head they're either uneducated or they're just ignorant."*

Knowing who you are as a teacher, and knowing about your local context will help with accepting and being accepted; it's two-way respect. This participant emphasised listening, which also requires clarification. Really listen, pay attention, use active listening and ask the student if you have heard them correctly. Respect is mentioned so frequently by participants that it needs some clarification. It requires using a respectful tone, empathy and being aware of our own emotions, and not allowing those emotions to impact a discussion.

The participants in my study valued education for their children, but not at the cost of their self-worth and cultural strengths. A parent described this as, *"If a non-Indigenous person raises their voice to an Indigenous kid, they're going to yell back, and part of that is because of the history."*

A school leader said her boys coped differently. *"My boys are very culturally aware and, if anything, they would stand up for what they believe in culturally, and would get in trouble because... it is like backchatting the teacher pretty much. So, most times they just sit there, shake their heads and shut their mouths... They would ask me. They would hold that question till the end of the day. They will probably just take it on the chin or whatever and come back to me for clarification and I would ring someone from home just to double-check am I on the right track?"*

I have seen communities that are strong in culture and traditions that take teenagers from other communities to help guide them into adulthood, and I have learned that our Indigenous cultures have much to offer us in terms of humour, resilience, connections to the land and to each other, and forgiveness.

What teachers can do

Teachers may not realise that they come with 200 years of colonial history sitting on their shoulders, which may cause problems with children. I was in my 40s when I learned the true history of Queensland. When teachers understand true Australian history and who they are as they present to students, they are more likely to approach students with understanding. Imagine if we were invaded by Martians, who took our lands and children, restricted our cultural expressions, controlled our lives and made us live like Martians do. Two generations later, would we be feeling resentment towards the Martian systems of domination?

Be aware that you do have a culture and that it differs from some of your students. Historically, education has been a way to replicate colonising attitudes and keep Indigenous people excluded from succeeding in equal ways. The breakdown of traditional systems and supports have caused transgenerational trauma that impacts today on families and children. Students in schools may be struggling as a result of that trauma (Atkinson, 2002a, 2002b).

All staff should approach Indigenous children with respect. Also, be aware that a response from a student may be based on the history of Australia and not a personal attack. Remain calm. I spoke to a lovely young man who was excluded from a school because of socks – yes, socks! He didn't have the right socks. A deputy would start a conversation by yelling at him. He got his back up and yelled back, which led to suspensions and eventual exclusion. That could, of course, have been easily remedied.

Cultural and historical awareness

What Indigenous participants said

Many participants mentioned that teachers need cultural awareness to be working with Indigenous children. *"At least they'd need to have a grip on that and not just a crash course, a couple of hours, because that's just a waste of time and I find... when you're an Aboriginal person and you see people working with Aboriginal children, and you look at all the criteria in their job description that they had to do to get that job, you think, where is their experience? They don't have any."*

An example of cultural awareness was mentioned by a liaison officer when talking about teachers who may have less success with Indigenous students. *"They're probably just not as understanding with them. They think that this is how it is at school; this is how it is at home. Not having that understanding... and especially, for example, like, for the Torres Strait Islander children if they have time off for tombstone openings... so that's lacking in understanding of the culture as well. Some, yeah, like obviously they are upset that the child is not at school and is missing out on work, but understanding that that is a priority for the culture, no matter what. Death and things like that is a strong part of their culture. And it doesn't happen once, it happens, the funeral and then the opening, it's ongoing. So, without that knowledge, [the teachers might judge the kids for being away] or the families."*

She went on, *"Americans can talk about and go on about their ancestors and that. For them, that's like generations and generations. We've got people alive today that can tell the story and then we've got people telling us to get over it... I like to wear Indigenous clothes all the time... wear the colours and be out there. And just for, yep, we're here, you know. We've survived. I don't know, I think when you come from families which obviously, they are alive today and these are in a lot of these children's homes. You know, so these kids are going home to their families, which will have experienced the same thing [stolen generations]."*

Having some understanding of the families and their histories will help staff to act appropriately in the cross-cultural space. At a conference, a well-known Indigenous academic advised that non-Indigenous researchers should break bread with her people for 15 years before thinking they could understand the culture and conduct research in an Indigenous setting.

A teacher said, *"Cultural awareness [is] not just about [our town], but about every single student and their culture because all these students here are not [local] like, they're different altogether. Because Australia's got hell of a lot of Aboriginal tribes. That's them all there [pointing to language areas map]. So, understanding that! You've got Elders from... so they can also educate new teachers as well. So, cultural awareness and definitely... that's where [experienced teacher] comes in, and a bit of mentoring from her."*

Some students may not identify as Indigenous. *"They need to know that, firstly, although a child may look Indigenous, they are not recognise[d]. That's a big part, so they may not know much of their culture, which a lot of adults are going through with the stolen generations. Or quite the opposite, they may have a fair-skinned student who know[s] quite a lot about their culture and may be happy to share."*

When mentioning the different Indigenous cultures in Australia, a staff member said, *"I think it's important to know things like, it doesn't matter what your cultural background is; as soon as there's a parent and a child, whatever their cultural background in their family is, it's gonna be different. Or you can have everybody from the same language group in 10 houses in a row and a house [is] gonna be different with the way that parent..."*

A teacher would tell new non-Indigenous teachers to the school, *"about all the distinct Indigenous cultures that we have within Australia. That each one is different. They may all be Aboriginal, but they come from different communities, they come from different areas. They have their own rules, they have their own values, traditional system and, you name it. So, trying not to generalise."*

Participants suggested that teachers learn some of the real history of Australia and their local area. *"[Teachers] definitely need to learn a bit about history, 'cause there are people that know stuff but actually really have no idea; and yeah, they like to think they do, but..."* and the speaker suggested acknowledging the Traditional Owners because, *"I think Indigenous people want to be recognised and accepted, and just the recognition that they were here."* Further, *"[Historical hurts] are very real and very recent. They [stolen generations] are alive today and these are in a lot of children's homes. They were taken from homes and made to do this [education] and made to learn, and it was probably against their will. So, for them, they probably wouldn't be able to sit and tell their child, 'Yeah, go to school because it's good and do this', because they've had bad experiences."*

What teachers can do

One way to increase self-awareness would be to learn about the Aboriginal and Torres Strait Islander cultures of the students in your classes. Visit cultural centres and research local histories. You may be surprised by what was missing in your education. Share your cultural background with students and teach respect for the cultures of others. Invite cultural experts in to educate students about the local area, sharing local knowledge. Learn how to approach Indigenous visitors and families, and how to show respect.

Understand that world views may be different

What Indigenous participants said

Having different world views was mentioned by staff. *"You know, even our world views, they're different, I don't know if all Indigenous families, like how education is, you know, how for other cultural groups, education is IT!... It's other things in life that are important. Education may be just one of the things we have to do."* Further, *"Instead of thinking that everybody else is like me, understanding that there might be people who're not like me."* The value placed on formal education may vary across cultures.

The life experiences of each person may lead to different perceptions of events. *"Like I had a friend that said about Prince William and Kate coming, and then there was Indigenous people that were protesting, and obviously on Facebook. Social media's the best. She's a good friend of mine, and she goes, 'Ooh, don't get me wrong. I have Aboriginal friends, but I get sick of every time an event happens and everyone's out protesting and carrying [on], and it's just a joke. Why have they gotta ruin my day?' And I said, 'You've just had a child, what happens in today's society. English come over and took your baby and say you're in your 20s now. Say you're in your 70s and 80s and the English people come over and everybody's cheering and going, "Hey, yeah!" and then poor little old you, standing at the back going, "No! They're the ones that stole my baby!" or something like that.' I said, 'Wouldn't you feel hurt inside? Are you gonna stand there and wave and cheer with everybody else? What would you do?' And she said, 'Yeah, I would probably be the one protesting as well.' I said, 'Exactly! That's how you need to see things; don't just criticise and judge and say, 'Oh, why do they always do this?' But actually look at it and say not as in 'why,' but as in the question, 'WHY?' Like, what's the reason? There must be some reason behind it."*

Taking time to learn about the history and cultures of your students is paramount.

What teachers can do

Due to differences in upbringing and resultant habitus and cultural capital (Dalal, 2016; Houston, 2002), teachers may see events and the world differently from their students. Teachers can listen with respect and humility and increase their wisdom.

Colour-blindness

What Indigenous participants said

A teacher aide gave an example of colour-blindness disadvantaging Indigenous children. *"I was in a prep class at [other school] and there was only three Indigenous kids out of 24 in one of the prep classes I was in. And she just kind of treated them like all the rest. But I can tell that they were having trouble listening and paying attention. So, I guess just like, trying to understand that they have difficulties and [also] like paying attention."*

Another example was a mainstream non-Indigenous Maths teacher who didn't succeed with an Indigenous teacher aide when she was a student. *"I guess that she thought that we'd keep up. Most of the kids in the class, like we had about probably four or five Indigenous people, and all of us struggled. We all sat together, and we tried to help each other, but [the teacher], it was in Maths B, she just thought we could keep up, but I failed a lot… She wouldn't really check on me unless I put my hand up, but I don't want to do that."*

A teacher explained how she tries to tell her pre-service teachers to be aware of that. *"And I always explain to my teachers, especially my prac students, you know, that these kids come from different backgrounds, you've got to realise that. Even though you want to treat them like your own children, you know that's a good way. There's still that boundary, that's cultural."*

This relates again to field habitus and capital. If teachers treat all students the same, they miss the opportunity to recognise how students come to this context with different habitus and capital, so different expectations will need to be taught, and student strengths should be celebrated. Student behaviour may need to be supported accordingly.

What teachers can do

A popular misconception is that treating all students the same is all that is needed. My critical review of current programs and research in Queensland showed that 'colour-blindness' exists in the locally supported behaviour support resources. Cultural differences in behaviour support have been ignored, yet treating all students the same is not appropriate. Treating all children the same can result in a mismatch of understanding and an increased suspension and exclusion rate of Indigenous children. Teachers can continue to grow in awareness of their cultural biases and colour-blindness in the classroom.

Curiosity

What Indigenous participants said

Participants said it is important to be respectful of Indigenous children if they are in your classes. Inappropriate curiosity and putting them under a microscope so that you can learn about their culture is not welcome.

One teacher said, *"Now kids tend to be put under the microscope in terms of when non-Indigenous want to find out about Indigenous issues, too much under the microscope. Where they are over-questioned. And I know that a couple of teachers here, they tend to do that, and the kids wanna just back off and they shut down. They don't want to say any more and that's understandable because they're just put under the microscope... So, that's a turnoff for our kids, I know that. And you have got to be very sensitive with issues and that's for all students across the board, you know. Black, white, you name it. But particularly when it comes to cultural, yeah. Even some of the relief teachers that come through here [do] the same thing."*

What teachers can do

When students trust you, they will tell you things about themselves. Singling out the sole Indigenous child only during NAIDOC Week can also be disrespectful. There is a continuum with one end being uninterested in the cultures of children, and the other end being curious to the point of being disrespectful and making children feel uncomfortable. If teachers follow the advice of local Indigenous staff, family members and Elders, they will be able to learn about the cultures of their students in a respectful way.

Attitudes from theme 1

The lists at the end of each theme show attitudes and/or strategies. The list below shows items that relate to your understanding of your place in the history of Australia and the effect of colonisation on your students. If you are struggling with these concepts, reading further into Bourdieu's habitus, field and capital may help.

Attitudes

✔ I am able to support the behaviour of students who have a different cultural background from myself.

✔ I understand that students may resent being told what to do by a teacher from the mainstream culture due to their history of colonisation.

✔ I understand that parents of my students may have bad experiences of school.

✔ I commit myself to learning about the history of colonisation in my local area.

Reflection

One of the most poignant memories I have in my learning journey was being the only foreigner on a bus in Hong Kong. I was travelling to the airport on my way home. I had only been there a few days staying with friends. I did not speak any of the language. I noticed that everyone left their bags in a common area and did not watch them. Theft didn't happen! I approached the driver to ask a question about where to get off and he ignored me. I am not sure if he spoke any English or thought I was being disrespectful in some way. That was an immersion lesson in the fact that I have a culture, and that it is not the same as everyone else's. Also, that I needed to show respect and learn some of the language and ways of showing respect. I have immense gratitude to my Indigenous friends, mentors and past students who have kindly helped me learn about their cultures.

I have gained much respect for Indigenous coming-of-age ceremonies and expectations around them. This has been part of my learning. I was also able to mentor girls through our senior formal milestone ceremony. I found an amazing boutique owner and took the girls dressed in shorts and thongs. She treated them like princesses and significantly dropped the prices so that each girl bought a dress that suited her.

As I planned my first formal, I felt initially like I was planning a formal standing on sand that shifted beneath my feet. I panicked but learned to go with the flow and ease my need to control the process. I could not tell exactly how many guests would be coming or what time events would happen. I learned to trust that there would be a good outcome and let go of my Western need for strict control. A dance troupe from the Islands came to celebrate the graduation of one of their young men one year. The performance was outstanding, and all the kitchen staff came out to watch it. I learned much about my own habitus and cultural capital, and that they were not always the best way. I learned to value different cultural capital and habitus.

Theme 2:
Knowledge of students and their cultures without a deficit notion of difference (bias)

" Bernstein's failure of reciprocal understanding: 'If the culture of the teacher is to become part of the consciousness of the child, then the culture of the child must first be in the consciousness of the teacher.'"

(Bernstein, 1970, p. 347)

Why learn about your students and their cultures?

Using Bourdieu's theory, when we come from different cultures (fields), we learn different habits (habitus) and knowledge and strengths (cultural capital). If we only see the world in terms of our experiences, our field and habitus, we may misunderstand the actions of others and not value the strengths or cultural capital that children from other cultures bring to the classroom. We may also judge others for not possessing the cultural capital that we possess. This theme fits in the larger picture around the classroom in the TASSAIS Themes graphic on page 6.

What Indigenous participants said

As well as learning about the history of the local area, participants suggested that teachers should learn about the particular cultures of the students they are teaching.

One liaison officer said, *"Like cultural awareness class or some items, just to break it down to them, so they will understand how black kids think... They need to know how they think, and how they act, and what they like and what they don't like. Like, some kids, when they get their mind overload, they are not interested anymore. Too [much] information, they don't like that if you keep on repeating the same thing."*

Staff and parents stressed that you can't generalise with behaviour and need to know that student. *"Yeah, just because they're all Aboriginal or all Torres Strait, they're still very different. They [teachers] need to understand that 'cause that's part of cultural awareness,"* one teacher said.

A secondary student relayed, *"From my understanding, he or she has to get used to the kids first. Like where they are, where they come from, what kind of culture they have and [some] of their personality, and learn a little about how expectations at home may differ from school."*

A primary school student made a suggestion that has stayed in my heart; a new teacher *"needs to know what we do and what we sing and talk about and what kind of songs we sing. Because our culture is about the animals that we want in our arms and all that."*

Some teacher aides mentioned that students may have issues at home and that teachers need to be aware that this could be the reason for behaviour. Knowing what students are experiencing and how to support them is necessary.

One teacher said students were going through *"this struggle for [their] own self-identity. You know, at that age you've got to know who you are and where you are going. And have some idea, and also with key people in place to say, 'Keep coming. You're right! Yeah, you're working all right.' Or 'come on,' you know, and 'you'll get there.' But if you don't have that support at home and you come to school, and you struggle in school and you don't have that support in school also, then you're a number of many that fall through the cracks."*

A liaison person related that students would say, *"'Teacher doesn't listen or understand us.' The teacher will probably flip and doesn't know what's going on and all these kids [are] sent to the principal; not knowing the back story because, like I said, you can't have a certain person sitting next to a certain person. You've got to know the community."*

A liaison officer said that at school, *"School is school time. Everything have to be on time... [A student may think] like 'I'll do it,' but you'll wait maybe five minutes."*

Another liaison officer said, *"It might be very hard for them to adjust between the two."*

Meanwhile, a boarding student stated the difference between home and school. *"[At home], we don't get in trouble if we ask to go somewhere but we just have to be home before dark, but when we're at school things have got to change."*

Often, Indigenous cultures place great value on ceremonies, and these are more important than schooling. One parent said, *"When it's like our family business time, which is like a grief in the family, a loss, they'll be absent for sure because we take our funerals very seriously. And regardless that they're children, they are still expected to be at funerals, especially if they're really close. Sorry business time is real important. It's a matter of a teacher working around them, you know, with loss of lessons and stuff."*

What teachers can do

Learning about your students and their cultures is paramount. Information about your community could offer insight into situations that relate to behaviour. Keep in mind that my suggestions may not directly apply to your setting. Local Indigenous staff and community can help you to learn about your students. Learning about local ways to show respect and adapt will go a long way. If you need to visit a home, take a liaison person with you. If you speak to family, start with a general chat before going into business. Appreciate a joke and have an open heart and sense of humour where possible. Be prepared to learn and appreciate differences. It would be arrogant to assume that your way is the only way of doing things. Be prepared to learn and appreciate differences.

Students suggested that teachers learn how students are related to each other. Some students from communities or certain families may not be allowed to sit together. The woman who followed me as assistant principal at the Indigenous school asked students to draw or help draw a family tree so she could understand those relationships. This showed a level of empathy and proactive work to understand relationships. Teachers should get to know students without a deficit notion of difference; this will mean becoming aware of your own cultural biases. Ongoing cultural awareness training was seen as necessary.

Teachers should also know, or be willing to learn, about differences in cultural practices, for example:

- Linear time – time can be seen as circular, and relationships are more important than linear time. If you invite an Elder, they will come but may not see linear time as you do.
- Family connections – get to know who is connected to who in the community. Learn how relationships are different. For example, an aunt in a Western family may be called 'sister' in an Indigenous community.

- Traditions and traditional knowledges – employ some traditional ways of learning in the classroom. Understand that ceremonies will take precedence over schooling and work around these.
- Learn some of the local language, or some Creole/Kriol – this will show respect for the cultures of the students.
- Be able to identify the Elders and Traditional Owners of a community group.

Expectations for behaviour may be culturally different

What Indigenous participants said

A school leader, when talking about her own children, said, *"It [was a problem], because it's where all my children are very proud of their heritage. Very much proud and for them to go to an all-white school, Catholic school, like that is very daunting for them, so having to code-switch is a problem in many ways. So, I guess the colour of their skin and the way they interpret things which they are pretty good at now. Before it was a big eye-opener. So, I don't know about any other kids, but it was the code-switching there had its ups and downs. Like a teacher might say something and they misunderstood 'cause it is different."*

Bourdieu's notion of field and habitus is relevant here. If we assume that all children will come to school knowing what we know, we are putting them at a disadvantage. Children will bring their strengths, and these strengths may be culturally different. Children may need to code-switch for language and behaviour to adapt to the different context.

A liaison officer also described how children must learn to code-switch for behaviour at school. *"I think a lot of kids, too, and even myself like, they don't like the whole sitting in the classroom and textbook learning thing because culturally it's all about song and dance, and hands-on, being out and learning that way. Even though people say, 'Oh, it's the new age and you need to get on with it and just be like everybody else.' But I think sometimes that culture, even if it's not taught to you, it still burns inside."*

Staff talked about sitting still. *"Being made to sit down for a length of time, you know, like at home you don't have to sit for periods of time, do you? You can get up and move around."*

A student also talked about not being able to walk around when they wanted, and having to keep their shoes on at school.

One Aboriginal liaison officer from a different community explained that her role was to teach students how to navigate school. *"They [students] learn our [community] ways and then they come into here, they have to learn white ways... school ways,"* she said, and went on to explain that at school, students will need to respect staff they do not know, whereas at home this was not an expectation. She taught the students to use "thank you" when food was served because that was a different cultural expectation. *"We talk to them about the teacher or other staff, in the kitchen, the dining hall when they serve you food, you say thank you... Different from home."*

I offered that a teacher may misunderstand and think the student was being rude, and the liaison officer agreed.

Further, at school, students needed to ask to go to the toilet. The liaison officer continued, *"They are coming into, like, two worlds; they have our world and the white world... They learn our ways and then they come into here, they have to learn white ways."*

Non-Indigenous staff need to understand cultural differences and how Lore may affect student behaviour. The liaison officer and another staff member went on to explain some of the Lore. Teachers need to know *"how we are related to each other"* and *"moieties and totems and clans... especially some of that boy-girl stuff"*.

As an Elder in her community and an experienced liaison officer, she also saw her role as helping new teachers understand cultural differences as they learned about their new teaching context, because this school may be different from their previous experiences in other schools. Teachers needed to know and understand some Lore. For example, some family members may not be allowed in the room with others. Students may need time to adjust to behaviour expectations at school.

A teacher in a boarding school also suggested not to nitpick. *"'Cause a lot of our kids come from communities where English is their third, fourth language."*

It could be considered disrespectful for students to make eye contact. This was emphasised by a teacher aide, *"A lot of teachers like a lot of eye contact, which is good, but in the Indigenous, they don't like making a lot of eye contact either."*

Indigenous children often have more autonomy than others. At home, times may be flexible, going to bed or dinner times may vary, staff pointed out. Children may not have a routine when eating, and they may do what they want at home. *"In the community, you'd be able to talk whenever you want to talk. Learning that difference from home and the way we do it at school,"* a teacher aide pointed out, while a liaison offer said that, at home, a behaviour *"might be something so small, but at school it is like a massive thing".*

A staff member said, *"They may get away with back answering at home or always trying to have that last say because the parent may not be strict with that. Whereas at school, that's something we try not to let the children get away with when they're spoken to, so that's where they need to leave it."*

Sex education may also need to be conducted in a culturally respectful way for some students. A liaison officer explained, *"You talk to the girls in like a group. If you talk to the girls and boys together, boys can get hurt. If the girls [are] in the class with her brother, they can both get hurt and [the] brother can stand up and say, 'Hey, I want you to go out.'"* In a situation like this, or at other times, a student may use behaviour to mask the real reason for them needing to leave the room.

Learning to respect Elders was mentioned by several participants from both Aboriginal and Torres Strait Islander cultures. One staff member said, *"Respect for Elders is pretty much so strong in my culture. It's very much still strong in my family [Aboriginal]."*

Another staff member said, *"When we go somewhere, I just tell them, 'You have to respect Elders, you know, 'cause they're important to you.' With their grandmother, you know, she's still alive. We go and visit her, and she tells them, you know, Torres Strait Ways."*

And another Aboriginal staff member said, *"I always tell my kids to respect their Elders, respect your own family, respect your brothers and sisters, respect to culture."* Please note, 'Elders' in this case has the traditional meaning of an Elder in the community. Automatic authority and respect may not apply simply because you are more advanced in years. Respect for teachers must often be earned by the teacher.

Parents listed some cultural differences in the way students behave, and said, *"Well, that's just common knowledge... the protocol that the older sibling looks after the younger ones. If there is a conflict, the older one will always be involved, because in our family they have to protect the younger ones."*

Touch may differ, as one parent said, *"A lot of children, they're really touchy. So, they like, you know, the closeness of holding hands, you know, maybe touching their hair. They get a little bit clingy sort of thing, but that's just their way of building a relationship."*

Culturally, students may be more aware of body language than teachers realise. They will be able to read the teacher's mood and expressions. They may also communicate through it, with the teacher being unaware of how something may have started. A parent who was also an office worker stressed, *"Unless you're aware of the body language, the facial expressions, it can be hard to... yeah. I mean I've walked out and probably because I've grown up in an Aboriginal community, you know, I've walked outside, and I've noticed straight away that there's two boys giving each other the eye... The body language, that may be hard to learn, though unless you're actually with, say, our kids quite a lot. I would hope that our boarding staff would be able to pick up on it a lot better, because they're, you know, right in there with the kids."*

Students will also read your body language. My partner died from cancer while I was teaching, and my group of Year 10 girls did not need to be told how I was feeling. They could tell. A parent suggested, *"Learning to read, you know, some of the body language. A lot of kids in the community don't know how to speak. They talk with their hands and gestures, and they can say a lot just by movement. So, they'll have, you know, a signal to fight. They'll have a signal for lots of things like that."* A teacher could *"sit back and you can read facial expressions if they're talking to each other just through facial expressions or body gestures. But you'll pick up after a while and go, 'Naaaah.' You know? It's all good there, it's not rude or inappropriate."*

One teacher said, *"Our customs and tradition is influenced through actions more so than words, so, for example, if something that's not right and doesn't sit with me, we either give each other the silent treatment or it's the facial expression. I guess that's similar to a classroom as well 'cause when something doesn't sit well with you, you either usually frown or shake your head in disbelief, you know? That also shows a bit of, 'You gotta stop what you are doing and change it, fix it.'"*

Another teacher said, *"Sometimes it's in the way the teacher speak[s]. You gotta be careful how you speak, 'cause a lot of our people, they can read body language, and they can read people's tone of voice. Change the way you talk, too."*

There has been a breakdown of traditional learning in some communities and families. A school leader explained, *"I think part of that is, if there's been a breakdown in the traditional knowledge system, where there's key people that are showing them the correct way to behave in the cultural Lore been no Elders involved in their upbringing, you know? And they stay disconnected, and they struggle between who they are and where they stand. [Example behaviours are] defiance, defying authority figures, not wanting to be told. [These come from a] breakdown of culture."*

What teachers can do

When discussing differences between cultures, staff related that adults may not have been pressured into going to school when they were children themselves. This past experience may be similar for their children and influence how families respond to school and the formal protocols of school. Teacher recognition of this difference in sociohistorical context may help to understand student behaviour.

Teachers need to understand that ways of teaching behaviour may differ at home. We can't assume that all children are raised the same way we were, and we should come to this understanding without a deficit view of other cultures. Teachers seem to accept that students may need to code-switch for language but may not understand that students may also need to code-switch for behaviour. Some differences may include the following:

- Students may be used to having more autonomy at home and likely will expect more autonomy at school. They may have to learn how the cultures differ.

- Students may be used to a relationship with adults based on a more equal footing.
- Students may have more responsibility than non-Indigenous families. Care for younger children, etc. could keep them from homework.
- Students making eye contact may be seen as disrespectful, especially during conversations about behaviour. There were also differences between home and school with speaking in public and "no eye contact", meaning that eye contact is not necessary at home when talking to children as opposed to teachers using eye contact as a signal that a child is listening and learning. Students may avoid eye contact, especially when talking about behaviour. Many non-Indigenous teachers are aware that Indigenous students may be reluctant to make eye contact, especially if they are being corrected.
- Be aware that students may read body language very well.
- Be aware of cultural differences around touch and sex education.
- For us, respect is equated with manners; for Indigenous students, it may mean something different, like, "I will be culturally and emotionally safe in your classroom." Respect from students may not be automatic; it may need to be earned by individual teachers with individual students.

Ways of learning behaviour may differ

What Indigenous participants said

A teacher, who is also a grandmother, explained how she was teaching this to her daughter as she parented the granddaughter. *"So, instead of 'don't touch,' I'm like, 'let her touch and feel what it's like, so just let her put, then she'll know then.'"*

Children learn from Elders, which is one of the reasons why working with families and communities is important. What a non-Indigenous teacher would call extended family may also be involved in children learning behaviour and in discussions after behaviour.

A teacher mentioned that family usually pitches in to 'discipline' each other's children. *"Like, my niece has got younger children. We all help discipline them."*

And a school leader said, *"[An] older sister is expected to make sure my brother's kids are all right… With the boys, when there's been need to have a chat, their uncles have taken them. They'll take them fishing and go and do something. And there's different ways, really, I guess. When you're disciplining boys and girls… with boys, they not really keen on the talk."*

Another staff member gave an example, *"So, that's a big part, but Owa [uncle] also has a very high place within our family structure, in our kinship system [mother's brother]. So, it's the maternal side, so my brothers are the ones who take my kids through ceremony, rites of passage. Because I have daughters, and I have no sons, they can't teach the men's stuff to my girls. However, they do run their birthday parties, and when it comes time for marriage, they are the ones that negotiate among the clans."*

A different staff member spoke about caring for younger generations: *"It's whoever is the next person that is capable or able to, and can look after them… or when something's been happening that they haven't connected, like the parents might be able and willing and all the rest of it, but that kid's not listening, so it's finding the right person that they gonna link to."*

A teacher explained how children may learn behaviours at home. *"That's cultural Lore. And cultural stuff. And they understand where they fit into their kinship system, but I don't just do it by myself. That also comes from the grandparents and Elders. That's a very big part of it also. The Elders and grandparents play a big part in that. And the teaching of Lore and the teaching of correct behaviour, how one should walk in accordance with the Lore L-O-R-E, cultural Lore. And how you treat others. Those are basics, but basics are very important."*

Another teacher said, *"Culturally speaking, yes [family does get involved in discipline]. So, we would have aunties, uncles, our grandparents involved. Even if they are in the same home, they will also do the disciplining. It wasn't as if they just sat back and watched. They're encouraged to discipline as well."*

A mature male liaison officer said, *"And sometimes, like when I say something wrong, the Elders will correct me and say the right thing. Yes, I respect the Elders. They're older than me."* I asked if the Elders hold the wisdom or the rules. He replied, *"Yes, always."* I asked, *"And teach the younger generation, even grandfathers?"* He agreed.

A female teacher with a Torres Strait Islander background explained that there were also gender differences in what was taught and expected. *"Boys would learn hunting and fishing, and girls would raise younger siblings, and you'd be within the house and the home, doing the female... household chores, cleaning responsibilities there, keeping your rooms clean, helping with household chores."* So, children may experience different requirements at home due to gender. *"So, if they [boys] were asked to do something at school where, see in our family we tend to think that that would be for the females. That could be a possibility [as a reason for behaviour]."*

Another liaison officer, a younger man, explained how respect was taught. *"Wow, respect! Knowing who is your Elder, by family tree line, family tree, the family tree. And just a general respect, you know? Like, he talk, I listen and vice versa. It is one of the biggest things I have, like growing up. Yeah, because you sit with pretty much your granddad or parent and they show you, what do you call it? A family tree? Yeah, pretty much because they're seeing how you show respect, and then from there, as I was growing up, I was seeing my mum and that, like all the Elders and that, and then she always tells me like, 'This is how you treat your Elders' and that... Yeah, listening's one of the biggest ones because they show you the rights and the wrong way as well. Yeah, because they've been down that track and they know the routes for... most of the way they teach is pretty much like a story, but they tell a story about 'This is what's the bad side [of] the story.' If you go down this track, then... and hear the other side of the story as well."*

Students may find it easier to learn through talking to a peer. A liaison officer said, *"Because it's easy to talk to the person next to you because you know... they can speak language as well. Because English is pretty much like a second language, and then we can just break it down if you don't know how to speak [English]. And it's very hard for me if I keep moving from home to city life, you know? It's pretty hard because I don't know that much English, it was very hard for me to talk to other kids in the classroom and understand the work is way different from back home."*

Respecting traditional languages was recommended by a teacher: *"If they [students] revert into language, we should accept that. Those are 40- to 60-thousand-year-old languages that are being spoken in our country for a very long time."*

A liaison officer explained how there are some differences in cultural norms: *"They quite often can go and stay for long periods with aunties and grandparents. That's quite the normal, as compared to non-Indigenous. Sharing clothes and food and not having their own. It's common to, I might wear their brother's shoes to school, or their auntie's friends, you know, it could be anyone's, so, not always bringing money, too, not always having as much money given to them, or certain things."*

What teachers can do

Teachers should be aware that how children learn behaviour at home may also be different from a school setting. At home, discussions about behaviour may take place while engaged in a task, and the discussion would be a general discussion of life, without sitting face to face and pinpointing the child with behaviour. That would be creating 'shame'. Learning may take place on country, with Elders and a cultural story, rather than telling children what you want them to do. One school leader likened it to telling a fable, and then explaining the message in the fable.

Children may also be encouraged to learn through experience, rather than being protected. If you are teaching small parts of something larger, which is a Western way of learning, you could show the whole and let children understand where the parts fit. Because students may be learning to code-switch for behaviour and other cultural situations, preparing them for new situations, explaining social conventions and allowing time to learn behaviours will benefit them. Children may be expected to carry responsibility more than in Western households. Students may then resent being treated like a child. I will suggest more in theme 6.

Why avoiding 'shaming' is important

What Indigenous participants said

A parent explained why avoiding shaming a student is important: *"This is probably something that affects Indigenous kids more than non-Indigenous kids [and] is singling out. If you single out someone because they've done something that they shouldn't have, in front of a crowd. Even if they were in the wrong. Just the act of singling them out seems to put them off forever. They'll never trust that person again. They'll never connect with that person. I don't know why? It's the shame thing. It is something that just affects Indigenous kids a lot more than, say, a non-Indigenous student."*

A liaison officer added, *"Well, it's an intimidating way. If someone's pointing at you, talking in a demeaning tone... and there's other people around, you don't want to be shamed... So, in that sort of situation, the shame is important, and they won't back down because of the shame as well."*

Several participants offered stories of what happens when students are shamed. *"When another teacher up here [in another class], when he was targeting a student, they would walk out and slam doors because that was the 'shame' factor then, you know. 'Cause I don't want to be put on the spot like that. Other kids will tease me later on in the playground."*

A liaison officer saw a situation escalate into a power struggle. *"Little things like, 'That's wrong!' – you know what I mean. I found that he shamed them. Or start pushing their paper away first. They would put it back, so he would push it back. Stop pushing them first."*

A school leader suggested *"not saying their name, unless it really becomes the thing [publicly] where I have to single them out or I'll go up to them".*

A liaison worker explained that *"kids don't want to be in front of the whole class. That's shame and it's not a good image for your Indigenous families. Shame is a big thing, you know? Like, we're shy, most are."*

A school leader was discussing her sons. *"Yeah 'cause saving face for the boys is very important. And the middle one is very much like his father, and that pride stuff is very important. And he's very different, I noticed, in [the] way that [he] would respond. Yeah, and giving the power to [them]; they are the ones that have the power to change things and put that right.*

Rather than they're feeling like they're being told [off] like a little boy, because that will only increase the anger and make them not actually do anything right. It will just make it worse."

What teachers can do

Harkins (1990) explains this well. I actually passed this reading on to a teacher who had shamed a student. I was in the classroom observing the teacher in a process that did not allow me to intervene. The student had her head on the desk and other students were trying to deflect the teacher's attention, but the teacher was determined to ask the student the question for the tenth time. That event sticks in my mind as an example of what to avoid.

Be aware that private interactions with some students will have a better result. Even situations where the student is being praised may cause 'shame'. You may lose ground with the student and need to repair the relationship. I would find a way to privately praise students until you know they are not going to feel shame if they are praised in public; and always correct them privately. There are many ways to do this; ask a student to come to you rather than call across a room; have a quiet chat or a private signal; speak later after the audience has left; or even a facial expression could quietly indicate your feeling if the student considers you a safe person.

Public shaming may leave a student no option but to save face in front of peers. If a student loudly exits a room, think about the situation that occurred before that. Was that student avoiding shame? Were they deflecting attention from someone else? Was there a cultural situation about which you were not aware?

Teacher lack of awareness can cause misunderstanding, leading to escalation

What Indigenous participants said

A school leader explained, *"Some of the behaviours that they're seeing may be culturally appropriate or culturally inappropriate, that what they're [teachers] seeing might not actually be as clear as just seeing as behaviour, but understanding culturally why those behaviours are happening. Kids not looking at you when they get in trouble. Not being confrontational, not wanting to be shamed in front of other people. Being closed off at times... Also, personal space issues and non-verbal, where teachers think they're rude, signs or gestures or even words that they use when they're not."*

A liaison officer also said, *"Yeah, using bad behaviours and knowing that, 'teacher doesn't listen or understand us.'"*

A liaison officer from a remote community who spoke 13 languages explained how a teacher's lack of information may lead to a misunderstanding of behaviour. *"The white people in the school can learn for like when the brother and sister sit in the classroom, they are [in] one class. A girl will ask the teacher to go to the toilet.' Teacher can't shout 'You can go to toilet in front of the brother! That's the main thing. Or the teacher can't swear or say rough words to the girl in front of the brothers. That's the main one... They can learn and respect our culture with respect to your culture, [each other]. But the white people can't have culture, only the Indigenous people can got culture."*

Hearing or vision impairment could cause misunderstanding. A parent said, *"If they can't read properly or if they can't, you know, like, kids go, 'Oh, what did you say?' 'cause they're half deaf. They don't put their hand up, and when they said it the [teachers think] they're being half smart, you know?"* He also suggested that teachers working with children who were *"half deaf"* need to be aware of that fact and not shame them.

What teachers can do

Cultural misunderstanding can cause escalation in behaviours (Partington et al., 2001). I was delivering training when a teacher aide gave an example. Some children had moved from an Island Indigenous school to a mainstream one. The early years children were used to all speaking at once, as they did at their previous school and at home. They were chastised for doing it with their new teacher, without understanding why. If we do not understand the reason for behaviour and cultural nuances behind a behaviour, we could unwittingly escalate events. We don't have to accept the invitation to an argument when we are invited.

If a child reacts to being taught or corrected, avoid escalating an event in a need to gain power over or win an argument now. Often later, without an audience when both parties are calm, a solution can be found. A liaison person or Indigenous staff member could help you to understand a situation. Learning from such a situation will help your increased understanding. Apologising to students may sometimes also be warranted.

Attitudes and strategies from theme 2

The suggestions that emerged from the research are grouped into attitudes and strategies, and are included in the lists below. Though some are specific, they indicate knowledge of your students. The most important resource in this theme may be local Indigenous staff who can help you to understand what is happening for students. Your Indigenous students may not share your understanding of time. They may need to have some control over their choices, and teachers may misunderstand behaviour.

Attitudes

✔ I understand that some behaviours I see from my students may be due to cultural differences rather than deliberate misbehaviour.

✔ My students may not need eye contact when listening to someone.

✔ I understand that students may need to see the larger context before attempting a specific task.

✔ I understand that the communication patterns in my classroom might require my students to code-switch from home language.

✔ I know culturally appropriate ways of showing respect.

✔ I need to learn more about Australian Indigenous cultures.

Strategies

✔ I make allowances for students having a different understanding from my own about time (more fluid and less determined by a clock).

✔ I give students a way to 'save face' to avoid 'shame' in awkward situations.

✔ I avoid singling out my students publicly for positive and negative reasons.

Reflection

This theme requires continued learning on the part of teachers. My daughter danced in a local dance company in a collaboration with dancers from an Indigenous community. The performance would start when the song man was ready after the smoking ceremony. The mainstream dance company adapted to a non-linear notion of time. The performance would start when the time was right by the song man, not 8.15 on the clock. That is one example of respectfully learning about time and not assuming that the dominant culture is the only way.

Also, I have come to understand that the word 'respect' has different meanings for different cultures. In my culture, it means that children learn to use the words 'please' and 'thank you', showing gratitude and having 'manners'. This is not a traditional part of Indigenous culture, and children attending schools may need to learn our expectations around respect. I learned from an Aboriginal man that shared property negates the need for saying 'please'. He saw it as equivalent to begging. I am also learning that 'respect' to some Indigenous people means something akin to "I am safe in your hands – you will value me and my culture". That is my interpretation, and I am happy to keep building on my understanding.

I worked in a school that was 100% Indigenous students, and the staff who remain for a length of time are those who have the heart for the children. After I had finished in my role as an assistant principal at the Indigenous school, a young man came to board with me as he needed support away from boarding school at that time. Being a teenage boy, he had hollow legs when he ate and I had raised girls, so this was a new experience for me. Half the meal that I thought would do for the next night had disappeared by bedtime. For his 18th birthday I took him to a smorgasbord restaurant, thinking that he could eat his fill that night. He didn't eat as much there as he did at home, and I learned that he was not as comfortable in the restaurant as he was in my home. I was still learning. I am still learning today. I left town to spend time with my elderly parents and work in another city, but the school remained in my heart. It still remains there.

Theme 3:
Connections with families and communities

"The AIEOs were adamant that many behavioural disputes involving Noongar students in the school decreased if they were able to spend more of their time working with parents and their children in a mode of prevention. A reactive approach focused on dealing with the students and their families after major incidents had occurred often prevailed."

(Gillan, 2008, pp. 213-214)

This theme fits with the first two as one of the larger picture in the TASSAIS Themes graphic on page 6. It is part of the bigger picture that sits around the classroom. Learning about local history and families is an important way to be respectful.

Connections with and support for families

What Indigenous participants said

A parent highlighted the importance of connection with families. *"Well, I reckon every teacher should engage the parents from the very start and try and build a bond there. Because that's like the biggest downfall of getting parents' involvement in a lot of school things. And then having them come in and, you know, talk and keep them included."*

One teacher recommended going through the *"right channels because there are protocols in place... When you say hello to the Elder, and he or she invites you to their family home for dinner or something, you can go."*

There are protocols in the community that non-Indigenous people can learn. As a behaviour support teacher in an Indigenous school, I would accompany a liaison officer as we visited families to talk about supports for students.

The importance of making connections with family was addressed by a primary school leader: *"I think it's very important to have open communication with families and to talk to them when problems start. I think you need to establish that and maintain that communication line the whole way through. So, you talk to them if things aren't going well, you talk to them about the strategies you've put in place and things you are trying to implement, and then you keep going, so I don't think that communication should ever stop. It needs to continue the whole way through. And then after that, [you could say], 'Oh, we've had a really good day today, so and so did this and this... I could speak to some families four times in one day. But that's what this job is, I think, and it establishes [and] maintains the positive relationship with families when they have faith and the knowledge that you're doing the best thing that you can do, and you've tried all these things before the problem escalates."* When there was a problem, this leader kept in frequent contact with the family. She had earned respect from the community and increased enrolment numbers.

A parent described a principal who worked well in the community. *"She's been in that community [in another state] for 16 years and she's had a lot of experience in Aboriginal communities. She doesn't have a magic wand, but she knows what she's doing, mate. She's made a lot of changes, like, making the school look different and introducing more staff too, 'cause when I was a teacher aide, they asked me if I could be one of the bosses and [with] all these teachers, we sat around and we had a talk about what the school should need. [What] should [we] have to [do to] keep kids at school? And we all said, 'yes, maybe a music lesson, maybe more sporting activities, more sporting gear,' 'cause at lunch break they'd just play under the big shed and there's not much they could do. So, we'd like to introduce a few more activities and, up in the old metal and woodwork, get that going again, 'cause that's my thing, as woodwork by trade. So that's been a talking process."*

I asked if the principal listened to the Indigenous workers. He replied, *"Yes, us, and we knew exactly what had to be there and what [was] not to be there."* This principal drove to meet families and connected with them.

What teachers can do

Teachers can communicate with families in a way that is culturally respectful. Ask your liaison officer how to do that. Email may not be suitable from a school to families. Learn who the families are in your local area. I always took a liaison officer with me when I wanted a behaviour plan to be checked and signed by family. We let families know that we were going to visit, and we did not go inside the house. We connected in conversations before beginning talk about behaviour. I dressed casually and followed the lead of the liaison officer. I suggest that you create positive relationships with families before needing to talk about behaviour situations.

I would also advise that when needing to talk about inappropriate behaviours with families, that school staff take an approach of working with families to support students. I know that these policies exist on paper, but in conversations it does not always happen that way.

Parents spoke of the need to support some parents who were having social problems which may be impeding their children's engagement. Often the community stepped in to help children and families in those circumstances. This reflected a holistic notion of pastoral care, which a school may include in their attempts to support families. In one school, a family had faced a disturbing crisis where a baby was due to be born. The mother was waiting till Grandma was paid to buy clothing and nappies for the new baby. The wonderful school staff filled the gap from their own resources. The donations were delivered to the mother in a culturally appropriate way, by a staff member who saw her regularly, had a close relationship with her and was accepted within her circle.

Parents involved with behaviour

What Indigenous participants said

One of the benefits of involving families with behaviour was that teachers might find out more about what was happening for students. A school leader suggested, *"So, actually asking [a] parent, what is it that you think might not be going right for your child here? What else can you tell me, you know, making sure that they're involved actively in problem-solving, what the situation is. The child might be presenting at school with these behaviours, and they may not have the skills to explain all of the trust or the confidence in the staff to tell them what's happening... So, by having family there and talking, and also the young person realising that school and family are working together. And that is not about being in trouble; it's about finding a way to support them, then it always goes better."*

She also talked about schools gaining the trust of families to be able to work together. *"The family feeling that there's a confidence, that you know, you are not just picking on my kid, you are actually trying to do your best. And yes, actually, this is a little bit more complicated than I thought as a parent and you thought as the teacher, and what we gonna [do] together?*

Because at the end of the day, it's about helping the young person engage and do what they need for learning."

She also suggested travelling family members to the boarding school to help the child feel safe, and see if we can resolve issues for the child. She described a young male who was running away from boarding school. The staff and mother put a plan in place. There had been some teasing in a classroom, and he wasn't sure what to do. *"Even just having a conversation with Mum, you see the way Mum talks to him, you know, and there's... I think in schools sometimes teachers have this perception, as soon as it's an Aboriginal or an Islander family, and as soon as they see eight or 10 kids or however many kids, very quickly there's value-based judgements happening, which can be on the mark, but they can also be so far off the mark that there's actually no real understanding of what's happening in their family. And why somebody's stressed out, running away or getting angry or upset."*

This school leader explained that Elders could provide guidance through *"telling stories, teaching the kids to play didg[eridoo], talking to them about the stories about how you behave, why things might go wrong, stories around the landscape and stories around seasons... When they're little they learn things, which are a bit like nursery rhymes, which tell you about the way things are. Oh, and sharing and looking after things, and then it comes about stories that you know when this is right. You look for the emu constellation, you can go to, you know, collect emu eggs and things like that... some wisdoms, and sometimes skills for living."*

Schools could use the Elders for guidance and structure reactive or restorative chats in a way that is culturally appropriate. A mother would use the chat with Elders in future discussion with her boys. *"Sometimes you gonna go back and talk to them about it, when uncle said this or that, you know, have you thought about..."*

In one case, a child had been teased by a family member, and staff did not know until they spoke with the parents. They designed safe spaces for him and his mum came in and walked through the spaces with him. This stopped him running to the road. They asked him what a good reward would be, and he responded, *"People saying nice, kind words to me."* Communicating with the family helped to explain the behaviour of the child in this way.

Involving family in behaviour helped to create a sense of safety for students and family. A school leader said, *"So, we travel parents in from communities to help 'cause I think when families are a long way away, they need to be able to see what's here, but also the kids need that safety, you know, when a young person is in distress, whoever the caregiver is, they need to have that person close so they can help. And so that the young person feels safe, and we can start putting things back together."*

What teachers can do

Teachers can talk with families about behaviour early, working together to support students. Talk frequently. Family may know more about the situation than you do. Students may listen to family more than they will listen to schools. Be aware that schools can be seen as perpetuating the dominant culture without consideration of cultural needs. Talk to families with humility and from the heart. They will see this. We can talk about behaviour the way that Elders would; telling stories, using metaphors and empowering children to repair relationships and learn responsibility.

I would avoid two strategies recommended by Marzano (Marzano, 2007, p. 144):

1. 'Overcorrection' – where the 'consequence' given includes more than the necessary actions in order to deter the student from repeating inappropriate behaviour.
2. 'Home Contingency' – listing all the inappropriate behaviours in a meeting with family and the student, giving the student right of reply (Marzano, 2007, p. 145).

I suggest that these are not culturally appropriate.

The importance of education

What Indigenous participants said

Most families value education highly. One parent said, *"We want them to learn. The parents here in [community] like every other school, the parents want their children to learn."*

The caveat is that parents were reluctant to put their children in situations that distressed them. The story of one teacher's own schooling experience illustrated that education did not come at the expense of cultural identity. She was singled out by her teacher for missing school for cultural 'sorry business'. Other students teased her, and she missed school for a further three months. Her mother did not make her attend because she knew it was hurting her, even though the mother had worked for the local court system and knew police.

This teacher recalled the experience: *"I didn't have to go to school if I woke up and I'd be like, 'I don't want to go to school today, Mum.' She'd be like, 'Yep, that's OK, go and do the washing for me.' I didn't go to school for three months in Grade 5. Three months straight. 'Cause I was getting bullied at school... And I lost heaps of school, and when I did go back my teacher'd be like, 'Where have you been, Miss [child]? You haven't been at school for two weeks!' And then when I'd say I couldn't come to school because Aunty or Uncle or Grandfather or somebody died, they'd look at me like I was crazy. They didn't understand. They had no idea whatsoever. And I was so embarrassed because I'd get asked in front of the whole class... and I think that's what made me a target of, you know, bullying... She could have just pulled me aside, but no! The nasty bitch asked me in front of everybody and embarrassed me. And the kids got on the bandwagon and then they started teasing behind her back. Sometimes in front of her and she didn't give a shit. She didn't care. It was like I could feel hate radiating off her. I hated school. So, three months I jacked up in Grade 5."*

Parents repeatedly stressed the importance of schooling for their children. They said, *"Education is important. We told them we're not going to be around, you know. When we're gone, you're on your own. So, we tell them to start thinking about the future."*

Parents wanted children to learn for their futures. They said, *"We need to keep on telling those children to go to school; and we need to tell [them] to go to school to learn, and if they don't go to school, they won't learn for their future, you know. I, myself, used to tell my children to go to school to learn; it was their future, so when they grow up, they might be special people."*

One aunty saw it as her responsibility to encourage her niece to behave while she was at school. *"If I was there with you, you wouldn't [be] doing that stuff, you know?"* she said.

Sometimes parents could be involved in settling problems. A community meeting might be called to help stop children fighting; even boarding school communities have come together to settle problems.

A mother related, *"They need time to think about what they'll do as they grow older. I try to talk to them, you know, tell these kids they need a good education. When you leave [school], it's time for you to go and look for a job. In the communities or wherever they come from. And you want to make sure they make us proud and the community proud. That they've been through their schooling."*

What teachers can do

We can be culturally respectful and understand that, at times, family and cultural business will take precedence over education. Create ways for children to catch up on what they missed. Learn about cultural events and value cultural knowledge and processes. I have learned that there are many strengths in other cultures that my own culture did not teach me: an ability to laugh at oneself, the value of family, and regard for the planet and natural resources. All of these I have learned to appreciate. Some of the best laughs I have had have been with my Indigenous friends around a food-laden table. Most families will value education, but not at the expense of a child's cultural identity. We can support them.

We can continue to work to remove barriers to education, and barriers to parent involvement, whether that is sourcing a washing machine or providing food, transport or extra time to help students gain cultural capital. A YouTube clip called *Swimming the River* explains how and why families can support schooling (Miller, 2014).

Overcoming barriers for families coming to school

What Indigenous participants said

The research was conducted in two schools. Staff in both schools discussed how families could be reluctant to come into the school for various reasons, such as transport problems or the lack of confidence with classroom activities (liaison officer, teacher, primary school leader). Therefore, they described strategies to involve families in school in order to overcome potential boundaries. One primary school planned whole-school fun events that involved families and required parents to bring their children. Transport was provided, if needed. Social events included time at the local pool, movies and themed evenings, to engage families and offer a relaxed setting for parents/carers to connect.

A liaison worker said, *"We want parents to come in. But a lot of the parents won't come in. But, then again, that's white as well. If you ask a lot of the parents to come in, they don't want to be involved."*

The reasons could be lack of childcare and appropriate clothing. One of the schools overcame this by creating an event each term for parents to attend. Children went home after lunchtime and came back with a family member.

The same liaison worker said, *"So, we make it really good, so the kids want to come, and they drag their parent, cause the parent has to come to it. (Children can't come alone.) There were fun activities planned and a casual time for staff and families to connect. We had a movie night. We got a lot that night, movie under the stars... (That's a good way to get the parents in.) Yeah, just to show their faces, too, 'cause sometimes [the kids] some on buses you know, you don't see their faces... And sometimes you have a little conversation with the kids, like you don't want anything heavy... and when you ring them up, they're easier to talk to. They're more accepting 'cause we find out we ring them a lot when there's a bad situation. But if you've already made [positive contact], like you're not their enemy, working together, they're more accepting when you ring them up."*

What teachers can do

Schools should create ways to invite families into the school. This can be less formal than mainstream parent-teacher interviews, which can be a daunting event for families, due to not having appropriate clothing, not knowing correct protocols, and sourcing childcare and transport. The interview data gave some examples of successful events.

One suggestion was to invite two parents from the class for excursions. The school leader recommended that the parents did not have to come, but they had to be invited. One primary school was attempting to set up a parents' room and playgroup sessions. A teacher in a secondary school suggested planning an afternoon tea and inviting Elders to come along. At the school where I work, the amazing staff will give of themselves to quietly support families as needed. This kind of support created lovely trust-based relationships with families that allowed for connections and joint work supporting children.

Attitudes and strategies from theme 3

Attitudes and strategies that emerged from the research are included in the lists below. No doubt as teachers grow in understanding, you will be able to add to this list of attitudes and strategies. You can increase your knowledge and understanding if you are open to learning from your local community, with an open heart.

Attitudes

✔ I understand that while most parents value education, they may reject school if it negatively impacts their child's cultural identity.

✔ I welcome parents into my classroom.

Strategies

✔ I create connections with families and carers.

Reflection

I have watched a young non-Indigenous woman teach prep at an Indigenous school. She developed from having minimal understanding of the culture to being a major link between school, specialist providers and home. She has gained trust and helped families engage with Western systems of diagnosis and assessment, explaining how best to teach their children. It is in the early years where we notice differences in the children. She always had the heart for the job, and with increased cultural understanding, has become a positive force for education in the families of the children she teaches. Her job is very challenging at times. A little extra recognition and support for her goes a long way towards boosting her energy.

One of the challenges teachers face, is that they may get a class settled and working in routines, and then gain a new student during a term. This child from prep Year 3 may not have had much previous education. One first-year teacher dissolved in tears as she explained this to me. The little girl had had about seven days of schooling and came into Year 3. She was not the last student to enter that class late in the year. Teachers do amazing work to support these children, as I support the teacher. Seeing this child's success is heartwarming. This is the magic that some schools can achieve for their students.

Theme 4:
Teacher qualities

"Staff need to know Noongar cultural practices and history before any positive change could occur."

(Gillan, 2008, p. 200)

Some teachers fare better than others teaching Indigenous students. After listening to the participants, I was able to identify some of the personal qualities that successful teachers possess.

The manner of the teacher

The teacher's approach when talking to students and dealing with behaviour were important. The subsections described here stress the qualities of the teacher that make up their manner to students. In the TASSAIS Themes graphic on page 6, theme 4 sits inside the bigger pictures and is related to teachers themselves.

What Indigenous participants said

Calm and friendly

Effective teachers make time for their students and are approachable. They *"respect [students] and give [students] a better attitude [towards teachers]. Have a good attitude towards them and show a little bit of interest in them, they'll gain the respect. They take an interest in students as [people]"* and *"build a bond".*

A teacher aide described her teacher: *"The kids come in and they feel comfortable. And they know there's no put-downs with her or [other teacher]. If you're struggling, that's fine, [as teacher aides] will all step in to be teacher aide and help. And there's no put-downs. And every time you make a step, you gain a step, and you're recognised for that step... And I sat in her class yesterday for half an hour... Supportive... Yeah. Very firm. [She will say], 'but this is, you know, we're moving on and this is how we'll do it.'"*

A secondary school boy described one of his teachers: *"He doesn't get angry. He just, sometimes he has his days, but everyone has their days when they're a little bit annoyed, but he doesn't tell us to do 100%, he goes, 'We'll give you a go at doing 85% or 75%. You don't have to be 100%, but at least achieve one of your goals.' He likes talking about goals and about our Lore and stuff like that."*

A primary school boy also said of one of his teachers, *"He's always happy every day and he makes me smile. Because when you walk into the class you see his smiley face, and when you go up and talk to him, he makes you smile."*

A liaison officer recommended that if a teacher arrived in the Torres Strait to teach, they should, *"Sit down and watch us, how we behave and all that, then slowly, they come a step at a time... to understand our way... and how to make us listen to them and understand them and work with them."*

One mother suggested, *"I think always smiling... kids will pick up if a teacher is genuinely happy or not."*

One father said that teachers should *"[h]ave a lot of patience... you gotta have that... and I guess just stick it out with them, you know"*, referring to perseverance. He spoke emphatically and with gratitude about the teachers who stuck around for his children.

Self-control is respected; another mother said that a less effective teacher *"would be emotional 'cause they would wanna chuck stuff at her".*

Heart

A school leader suggested that children will pick up very quickly if a teacher has the heart for teaching them. Other words used to describe good teachers were 'empathy' and 'compassion'. *"They speak to them in a really good way. And they are encouraging them to do their work but not with yelling or shouting."* They said that one teacher *"talked nicely and when someone did a mistake, she said, 'It's OK, you'll get it.' Like, when they're doing drawing and when it happened, she'll find them a new paper."*

Heart was also mentioned by another school leader: *"They need to have an understanding of cultural appropriateness. They need to have a good heart. They need to be willing to work with the school counsellor, like in a psycho-educational sense, have an understanding about trauma and neglect, and the barriers to education. Just willing to be open, and to ask the questions that they need to know as well and to get that support, so it's about new teacher starting but supporting them as they go through, which is really important."*

A liaison officer who described an early years teacher said, *"She's got empathy… she's got a heart for them and feels for them, and she's really compassionate."*

When asked about a particular teacher aide who could be short with the children, gruff on the outside, a liaison officer said, *"She doesn't rough-talk the kids. Yeah, she's got a good heart. And she really cares about the kids… when she's rousing at the kids, her heart's crying, she goes back and sees the kid and always say, 'I'm sorry.'"* This teacher aide was gruff on the outside, but in her heart she cared for students. The liaison staff appreciated this.

Humour

Several participants mentioned staff having a sense of humour. *"When they are all tensed up and working on Art, they could let a kid tell a joke so everybody can laugh at everybody's joke. And they think, yes, she wants to [listen] to jokes. So, say to one kid, OK, it's your joke this morning… Everybody have this laugh and teacher gets in the middle of the conversation or the teacher could even tell them a rhyme, like a riddle sort of thing, and they've got to work out what this riddle is. Not go in there and be all tensed up like, 'Oh, school's all about, I want to be the [best] teacher' sort of thing, 'cause you gotta get that respect in the classroom."*

Open-minded and aware of personal bias

Being aware of personal biases is important. You can find out more about self-reflection at llewellynconsultancy.com.

A liaison officer advised teachers to, *"Try not to be judgemental. That's the first thing, because people can judge somebody by just their appearance straight away, or their clothes or when they walk if they've got no shoes on or something."*

Another quality was being open-minded and not assuming they were always right. A teacher recommended, *"They need to be open-minded, culturally aware because there are many cultures here. Don't assume that you know, that you're always right. You know what else? Have a heart, be passionate. If you are not passionate and you are only doing it for the money, then you are in the wrong field."*

A liaison officer said she was, *"Trying to be a bit more relaxed and have a chat. Still getting the job done, but without coming down on them like a ton of bricks. And I think that they sense that. They know that. But while we're having a chat, they think, 'she's not yelling at me because I'm talking,' but then, 'we'll work through it slowly together.'"*

Being willing to apologise

A school leader recommended being able to apologise if needed. *"When teachers haven't worked in Indigenous education for a long time but are willing to see what's happening, what went wrong, and kind of apologise for their behaviour; I think I've probably only ever had two of those in my whole career and I always went back and it didn't feel good at the time. I'm glad that I went back and I explained my behaviours and what I did... and take responsibilities for what I did and how it escalated the situation, I think the students really respect that."*

Teachers learn that being willing to apologise to students goes a long way to building trust.

What teachers can do

If you don't want to read all the suggestions from the participants, I suggest that you read the previous section. These comments are about who we are as teachers – who we are as we present to the students. The first quality of successful non-Indigenous teachers is their manner. They are calm and create a sense of fun and even family in the classroom. They most definitely do not use an 'I am the boss' manner, but instead treat students gently and respectfully. I witnessed a young teacher approach children on a climbing frame that was not allocated for their age group. She said, "I am not sure if you know it, but your age group is not supposed to be..." Rather than yelling a demand from a distance, she approached the students quietly. Be calm and friendly.

It is difficult to describe having the 'heart' for Indigenous education. If you don't have it, the students can tell, and your job will be more difficult. If you genuinely care, students will sense that and, though they might test your resolve and persistence at times, they will appreciate it, and relationships will be easier. If you are just showing up for the pay, maybe choose somewhere else to work. In remote communities, children have seen teachers come and go for years. They become disheartened by this; I would be, too.

Being open-minded and aware of personal biases are qualities that will serve you well. Having and maintaining a sense of humour is a necessity if you are going to retain any form of sanity in any kind of teaching. Being able to share that sense of humour with students and share in their humour creates good relationships and a comfortable environment in your classes. Teachers should not shame students or use sarcasm or humour that students may not understand. They appreciate a teacher using self-deprecating humour and explaining humour to them. Also, directing humour at the whole class is better than at individuals. Tread carefully until you know students well, because it is the recipient who decides whether your statement is humour or a put-down/sarcasm. Being humble enough to apologise to students when needed brings you to a level of humanity and grace that creates an environment where mistakes can be made, and recompense sought. That is a great example to set for students as *you* learn.

Communication style and body language

Non-Indigenous teachers may not be aware of the cultural strength around non-verbal communication and being able to read body language accurately. Non-verbal communication is not common in mainstream Australian culture, so you may miss messages between students till you are aware of it. An issue could brew between students solely due to body language or a 'look'!

What Indigenous participants said

Participants spoke about body language as a means of communication. One teacher said, *"You gotta be careful how you speak 'cause a lot of our people, they can read body language, and they can read people's tone of voice. Change the way you talk, too. You gotta talk nice... I can be harsh if I want, if someone's acting up. But that's not all the time. Harsh all the time don't work. Yelling – that don't work."*

A teacher aide talked about a teacher who could read the body language of students to tell how they were feeling and then how to react to them. She would *"let them sit down and have some time out. Let them do what they want to do, like iPads or something, and then bring them around slowly. Once she's got the rest of the class settled and stuff, then she'll come back to them and do one-on-one."*

A parent said of good teachers, *"They speak to them in a really good way. And they are encouraging them to do their work, but not with yelling or shouting."*

Parents and staff recommended that teachers use language the students can understand when communicating with students. A liaison officer said, *"You can't go using big words and stuff that they don't understand."*

Another liaison officer said, *"It's like they change the way of talking and yeah, come down [in terms of language register when needed]."*

A parent also warned against using words that the children don't understand: *"Our kids are used to words that are broken down, like 'consequences'; some of the kids don't even know what it means... all these big words, they don't break it down and explain it. Like, they get taught it when they're getting taught themselves at [university] to become a teacher, but when you go into [a] community, because these kids aren't hearing these words all the time, it's hard for them to understand what the teacher is saying to them. So, the teacher might say, 'Oh, look, you're going to suffer the consequences,' and the kids are saying, 'What does consequences mean, Miss?' They break them big words down and explain to the kids."*

A teacher supported that. *"You can't go using big words and stuff that they don't understand. So, you've got to understand that these kids aren't philosophers or anything. They don't use massive words... [academic] levels are going to be all over the place."*

English may be a second or fifth language for students, so they may struggle.

A liaison officer said to speak to students *"[i]n a way that isn't so hierarchy all the time, to come down... to talk to them as a family would or to have that understanding of their culture, but cultural language also".* This refers to an attitude of superiority.

A parent described it as, *"With any Indigenous kids, you raise your voice, they're going to raise it back. A lot of Indigenous kids react better to other Indigenous people, as in teacher. When it's non-Indigenous, and they raise their voice, of course they're going to get a negative reaction. There are other ways, like, you could talk calmly to them, I guess."* This parent also recommended contacting parents.

One mother said that staff should also speak in a respectful way or, *"[t]hen the kids are gonna say, 'well, we'll talk back the same way to them'".*

A liaison officer said, *"Yelling does not work in class... they don't want to go back to class."*

If a teacher tells the kids, *"'Go out!' it hurts the kids,"* said another liaison officer.

Staff praised others who were flexible and able to negotiate; one example given by a teacher was, *"When you've finished [your work], you can mix your music."*

What teachers can do

Be prepared to learn about non-verbal communication and ask those around you for help. Students will read your body language and tone of voice, even if you are unaware that you are communicating in a particular way. Carl Rogers (Rogers & Freiberg, 1994) wrote about being congruent as a teacher. Who you are and what you feel on the inside should be consistent with the way you treat students, and your values and goals. If your values are misplaced or you are not congruent, students will know. Blackley (2022) talks about always starting with a 'Green Footprint'. Start every interaction with a calm, respectful and positive approach, and interactions will go better than redirection or an 'I'm the boss' attitude.

Learn some language

I won't go deep into the Maths of Rasch analysis here (Bond et al., 2020), but the results of the survey analysis revealed that the teacher learning some of the student's language was the least frequently used item by the survey respondents. It then emerged that teachers who actually endorsed this item were more likely to be more committed to teaching Indigenous students, and more likely to succeed with them.

What Indigenous participants said

A teacher quality that gained respect from students was the willingness to learn some of their language. A liaison officer shared her ideas: *"One thing I believe… to help with behaviour is just have that connection of understanding of language, even if it was to know a few words that the children could relate to, [for students] to have that more relaxed feeling, to have that connection with the teacher."*

A senior girl also suggested getting to know some of the language of students: *"But if you get to know the language, like, say 'hi' or 'bye' or 'where you going?', or you say something so awesome, everyone will turn and say, 'He did that!' and everybody [will] be like, 'Oh, my God, you say that!' and the teacher will be like so crowded with kids… If you're interested in the language, you are interested in them as well. So, [it's] better to know that, OK, this teacher [is] interested in my language and interested in my culture."*

A teacher said, *"On top of myself teaching them English, I also learned Yolŋu Matha. I also learned Warlpiri. I also learned Arunta. These are different languages my students have taught me, you know. So, I think the best thing about it is that, when you do develop that rapport, that line between which is teacher, and which is student becomes a bit hazy, a bit fun; fuzzy that you're learning so much from your own students. And you need to take that on board and learn from them, because at the end of the day, it's just you and the class, isn't it? And you're struggling to give the best possible learning outcomes for kids. And if it means you've gotta go the extra mile, then you gotta go the extra mile. I mean, we're not in it for the money, are we?"*

A male non-Indigenous teacher was highly respected because he *"wants to learn our culture, how we speak"*.

What teachers can do

Learning some local language or Creole/Kriol will show your commitment to the students and your willingness to learn. I remember trying to pronounce a word that the desert students were teaching me and them laughing at my attempts to get my mouth around a syllable. When teaching at the boarding school, I got to the stage where I understood most of the Creole/Kriol. This helped with understanding the reasons for behaviour. If I taught at an Indigenous boarding school again, I would have a map of the language areas on the wall and highlight where students are from. I would also try to learn to say "hello" in each language as well as a few other words.

Believe in student potential

A complaint in Indigenous education is that teachers expect less from students; that teachers may just provide worksheets or 'busy work', and as long as students were quiet, the teacher was happy – whether they were learning or not. I don't see this, personally. I have been impressed by the potential and achievements of students when they are given opportunities. My work points my focus to students who are struggling. Note that I firmly believe that Indigenous children succeed.

What Indigenous participants said

Staff expressed a need to believe in the potential of students. One secondary teacher suggested how a class 'community' could come together by supporting someone who was struggling. She described how she led students to help each other so that one girl could experience success: *"One of the things is that they were hesitant about [Joanna] coming in, and I say, 'Look, we need to work on her, we need to show her our way in the classroom, and hopefully she follows,' and they've been so patient with that girl."*

Staff also referred to teachers having high expectations of students. *"Raising the standards; not dumbing things down, with the Indigenous kids. And I'm certainly seeing that,"* a staff member said.

A parent complained that when her child had been transferred to a school down the road, he was put down a year. She said, *"Well, if you look at the [reading] program, have a good look at it and see where the kids should be sitting at the end of the day, they're not really right up to where their standard should be."*

'Busy work' like colouring in or relying only on worksheets is not seen to be productive for students.

What teachers can do

The vast majority of teachers put their heart and soul into achieving the best for their students, whatever their culture. It is just something to be aware of, that we don't let bias creep into our expectations.

Confidentiality

Sometimes students will trust staff with confidential information about families or their situation. The worst thing staff can do is betray that trust.

What Indigenous participants said

Some students discussed the need for teachers to keep student information confidential. A primary school girl said, *"If the kid wants it private, [keep it] private."*

A mother mentioned confidentiality and respect, talking about a teacher from her past who did not show that respect. She said, *"She wants to know everything, like; even if it's personal, she would want to know about it."* This was not well received.

Staff agreed, and one school leader said, *"Kids don't like it if you've been talking about their business... and kids pick up on that really quickly, I think."*

What teachers can do

While information gained may be salacious, and culturally surprising, keep it private (within reporting requirements).

Boundaries

You might think that some participants expected looser boundaries, but the reverse was true. This was my learning in my first week at the Indigenous school. As with all students, boundaries must be clear. When writing an Individual Behaviour Plan based on a Functional Behaviour Assessment, I like the humane approach that comes with 'be consistent with your inconsistencies'. This suggested the need to understand when to vary boundaries based on student experiences and life circumstances around them. The example I use is, if their dog was hit by a car this morning, we might be more understanding today.

What Indigenous participants said

Staff stressed that clear and strong boundaries were important. Students knew which teachers they could 'play up' for. Staff recommended being 'strict' and having a 'warm demeanour'.

A teacher aide described a male non-Indigenous teacher who was a good example. *"He will not hesitate to ask them to leave if they've been disrespectful or misbehaving... he's very much about praising them as well when they are doing good."*

That teacher said to students, *"If you want my help and respect, then you need to show me help and respect."* He also *"set the boundaries straight away when they come into class. 'Take your hat off. Take your earphones out, and here's what we're gonna do...'"*

In some classes, when students had completed their work, they could have free time or listen to music.

Students appreciated teachers who implemented boundaries. A primary school girl said, *"So, be angry at them if you have to be. Just make a point or something."* Further, *"But I think the voice, it needs to be – you need to really get it through to the kid's mind... if you need to step it up, just step it up."*

A primary school boy said this about his teacher: *"She cares and puts her foot down all the time."*

Parents wanted teachers to teach clear boundaries in the classroom; one mother said, *"And that thing where the teacher's got more control in the classroom than what the kid's got."* Also, that they should *"get on the situation before it happens [and] take that respect back in the classroom".* This describes a prompt response to solve problems while they were still small, and the teacher needing to implement the boundaries.

A staff member described a teacher who struggles as, *"the one that can't really get above the situation, I reckon. And a good teacher always stops the whole class and talks to everyone, saying, 'What's going on here? Why are you doing this, doing that?' But if you do that in front of a kid – sorry, in front of the class – it's a very bad image, and he'll keep carrying on because he got shamed in front of his peers, you know?"*

There is a difference between gaining respect and authority in the classroom for safety and learning time and being aggressive in communication style. A teacher described it as being, *"Angry, aggressive, abrupt, like you're talking over them. And sometimes it is OK to be a bit over. You know... but you've gotta have some leadership, kind of authority. Yeah, sometimes it just crosses that boundary. I don't know, like it just gets too aggressive. Like, I've heard some of the teachers from outside the room screaming, and then next minute the door opens and kids [are] out. I'm thinking, no wonder why. Yeah, probably got screamed at home, or other places, you know?"*

I am the first to admit that I have responded emotionally to student behaviour. My goal, though, is to remain in control of my emotions as I work with students.

A frequent discussion item for staff was having clear boundaries and teaching expected behaviours. These phrases were used to describe how to teach and implement boundaries: *"lay down the law"* (a teacher); *"explaining that it is not acceptable in the classroom"* (a teacher aide); and *"classroom structure covering rules and... setting the boundary between the teacher and the students"* (another teacher).

One school leader suggested, *"Talk to the kids about what our classroom should look like. Most kids have a good understanding of what's right and wrong generally, and set that up and [negotiate] what the rules are, and only [have] five rules and a good rule, but in positively framed words... The fact that a six-year-old can tell you that a reward is somebody talking to them in kind words, the kids have a good handle on it."*

A teacher related what she would advise new non-Indigenous teachers. *"I would say to them, 'Establish your boundaries; what is acceptable. Kids need to know that. 'Cause if you accept more, they gonna give you more. Like, if you accept less, those wrong behaviours, you'll get less.' So, I'd say to the new teacher to work hard. I think that's what [Jenny] has done. This is in Term 1; she's done all this work, you know, in time and effort. But the payoff is in Term 4. I mean, it's less [behaviour work]."*

A teacher aide related that one boy was interrupting a well-respected teacher while he was trying to read to the class. The boy was asked to go to the head of primary, while the class took a drink break. The teacher told the class, *"'Come back,' and then we were right... Rather than get into a conflict [with the boy], he [the teacher] said, 'let's have a break and then come back,' and that worked."*

What teachers can do

Setting boundaries is an important part of teaching. A boundary for a classroom could be described as the difference between behaviour that is appropriate for this learning setting and behaviour that is not. There is a difference between a boundary and an expectation. If students do not follow the expectation, then it is not a boundary at all. It is the job of the teacher to implement and follow through to create an actual boundary. It was clear in the comments by participants that in secondary school, the boundaries were implemented so that other children could keep learning. This is when staff other than the classroom teacher could help with chillout time and listening, allowing learning to continue for the other children in the class.

Staff also wanted to help remove barriers to learning for children.

Visit llewellyn-consultancy.teachable.com to help you create a plan for your classroom that will implement boundaries – search for 'Writing a Classroom Behaviour Plan'. The circle model of boundaries in that training explains it well. The reactive strategies section in the online training gives you a scale of possible strategies that go from minimal interruption to more intrusive for the learning time.

Gain trust and respect

Some teachers may find themselves in a position at the front of a room where students respect their position, but in most modern classrooms, there is no automatic authority, trust and respect; these must be earned. In all interactions in classrooms, trust and respect promote positive relationships.

What Indigenous participants said

A senior girl gave me some advice: *"[Students] don't have time to wait. If you want to do things, you do it there. If you don't do it on the time, you just slack and you just wanna slacken their emotions. They don't want to do it now. You told them to do it on that time on the spot. 'Cause you don't do it on that time on the spot, you letting them down. They're gonna be disrespecting you 'cause you did that... like if I say, 'OK, I see you at the library or shoot hoops,' they'll be there. They [are] standing there, and they don't [have] any patience."*

She went on to say that if teachers did let students down, *"they should apologise and find a way to do it immediately there as you are speaking to them".*

Also, students will go to people they trust. Teachers, teacher aides and school leaders also talked about teachers who were trusted by students. A school leader said, *"[He trusted her] enough to be able to tell her [what was happening at home]. If students don't trust teachers, they won't tell them what is happening and why they are 'carrying on.'"*

If staff can build trust with students, they will understand more about what is happening for those students. Having respect for students and their cultures was discussed in detail in theme 2. It is an important quality in teachers.

What teachers can do

Be aware that you are creating trust and respect; they may not come automatically. Act in ways that build trust and respect, and allow students time to learn that about you. I have asked students in mainstream schools before, "Have I ever treated you with a lack of respect?" They had to answer "No." Then I was able to ask for respect in return.

Blackley (2022) researched teacher decision-making and teacher-student interactions. Her Four Dimensions framework is a good place to increase awareness of your interactions and the impact they have on students.

Meet high expectations in the role of teacher

One of my senior girl participants thought her teacher did not take his job seriously. She thought that he was slack because he was teaching Indigenous students and didn't have his work ready. He was always apologising. She, quite rightly, expected more from him.

What Indigenous participants said

Students expected high standards from their teachers. A senior student was frustrated by a teacher who was fun, but also showed a lack of organisation, misplacing things and not *"doing his job properly"*. The students had high expectations of their teachers. Staff also discussed the high professional standards required by teachers. These included: being on time; providing high-quality work – as well as the need for teachers to expect high-quality work from students; and celebrating successes with them.

One teacher said, *"Having things up really, being prepared. You know, I like things like, first steps and those sorts of resources, stepping out because they have good structure, and they break skills down, which makes it explicit."*

A school leader spoke about visible preparation: *"When you go into those classrooms where a couple of teachers have – the day's there [visible], it's all planned out, so it's no surprise. They remind kids when it's coming up to transition, that things are about to happen. Having lots of visuals there for the kids, whether that's a visual timetable or something on the wall, so they actually know, and they're prepared. Model what you want to see and be well organised. Read the* What Works *books. They're a good resource."*

What teachers can do

Most teachers are professional and work very hard for the benefit of their students. It goes without saying that we should be taking our work seriously. Students will notice if we don't.

Not necessarily Indigenous

In the interviews, staff who were identified as being successful with students were not necessarily Indigenous. This topic surprised me, and I reiterate that this discussion came from the participants and was not planted in the conversation by me. Non-Indigenous teachers can be the right person for the job teaching Indigenous students.

What Indigenous participants said

Staff spoke highly of some non-Indigenous teachers and were critical of one Indigenous staff member. It was made clear that staff who were identified as being successful with students were not necessarily Indigenous. An experienced teacher who had taught primary and secondary school said, *"Just because you're Indigenous in an Indigenous school, or whether it's a workplace, doesn't mean you fill the seat well... you've got to come with the... knowledge, everything that goes with it."*

And a school leader said, *"It doesn't have to be an Indigenous person."*

A teacher spoke about non-Indigenous teachers who go well with the kids. *"They're more open to diversity, generally speaking... Accepting of other cultures. Open-minded as far as trying new things. Some people come set in their ways straight away and they don't want to change. Even the old school, you know. You can be still old school but try out new things. And more open-minded... They may be more passionate in their teaching as far as sensitivity, and all of those things coming through... Understanding the knowledge, everything that goes with it. So, I guess, in a way it depends on the individual. Not everyone can do the job properly, so to speak. Or be professional about it. It's sad to say, but there's good and bad in all of us and that's what it boils down to. It's much more related to heart and integrity than skin colour... So, whether you're black or white, not Indigenous or Indigenous, you have to come with the right mind, and in terms of mind, a good heart, so there's that sense of the issue that comes with it. Being open and mindful to others, respectful as well as integrity."*

A liaison officer said, *"And it's getting the right people to work with the kids and engaging properly. It would be good to have people with more experience that have had longer... Because as an Aboriginal person, we see it as, 'Oh, no, they're only here for the money because they didn't want to know us before, why do they want to know us now?' See what I'm saying? And they are putting gardeners on. They are taking Aboriginal gardeners away and replacing them with white ones. You know what I'm saying? And I'm watching all this and we're surrounding the kids with not the right people."*

There is no doubt that, generally, Indigenous teachers have an advantage. Staff spoke about whether teachers are Indigenous or non-Indigenous. Some said that, *"Aboriginal kids look up to Indigenous teachers and they would respect them more... 'cause a lot of Indigenous kids have respect for their Elders; you grow up with that."*

Indigenous staff may find supporting behaviour of Indigenous students easier. A school leader said, *"Culturally, that helps. It does, it helps."*

One teacher explained that advantage: *"I think I'm lucky because of my heritage. I'm lucky that I'm here teaching and I'm teaching my own mob. That's just down to luck for me. But I honestly think that if you build a foundation of good relationships between you and your students regardless of colour, and you can show that you trust well, then you've earned it anyway. You've earned respect."*

Parents explained that teachers did not need to be Indigenous to be good for students. I have worked with many highly successful and respected Indigenous teachers, and I have also worked with two who were not the best person for their students at that time.

What teachers can do

Whatever culture we come from as teachers, we can learn about the cultures of our students and become an effective teacher for them in the classroom. Reading my suggestions and adapting them to your local context with local advice, you can increase your cultural awareness.

Actions for teachers to avoid

During the interviews, there were suggestions about what teachers should avoid.

What Indigenous participants said

Children differentiated between teachers who were calm on the inside and *"angry on the outside"*, said one primary school boy.

"She just calm right through, you know," said a senior girl. *"You won't get negative vibes or anything like that from her; it's so calm."*

And those teachers who were angry all the way through, students did not like it when teachers *"yell... a cranky voice... and it's like... all crunchy-up voice; in an angry voice and he's yelling at you"*, said one primary school girl.

Students equate teacher use of negative tone to a dislike for them and a culturally domineering attitude. A primary school girl said, *"Because if she growls real loud, that means she hates them and she doesn't like them."*

Teachers and other staff who were not succeeding were described by a liaison officer: *"Like, even the teacher's aides and stuff are struggling a lot. I see that a lot. And they are in tears a lot 'cause they find that hard 'cause they don't understand what's going on."*

A student said (about one teacher), *"I feel sad that they're going to get in trouble, and I just don't like when Mr... gets cranky when there's only a little bit of good kids, and I didn't see them act out very bad."*

Students discussed relief teachers who did not go well with the students. A student mentioned one who would send students to time out without a warning. Also, *"they freak out more"* or they don't follow through on their consequences.

A teacher aide described a supply teacher whose attitude was, *"'I'm the boss, you're doing as you're told.' And that's why the majority of them don't like [supply teacher]. Because [he/she] goes in and this is what's got to be done and that's it. [He/she] goes by the books, whereas none of them want to listen... He needs to relax, like he's too uptight and thinks that this has got to be done, and it probably does have to be done, but you know, it's trying to get to know the kids a little bit more and... you have more success with them... so you give respect and they'll give respect back. Don't try and be their boss."*

A senior student also described that person: *"We don't focus for [relief teacher], you know, 'cause [he/she is] bossing us around. We don't like [him/her] ...And that's what I see in some of the classrooms. They don't like getting bossed around, so they'll sit there and do their own thing... they be smart arse as well, just joke around and don't really do the work."* This particular supply teacher in a secondary school was frequently mentioned as an example of an unsuccessful teacher in this context.

Four staff recommended that staff not use an 'I'm the boss' approach. This could be interpreted by Indigenous students as a domineering attitude that is resented. *"And not to have a superiority complex when you're around Indigenous people! Please! Those times were out, that was 30, 40 years ago, not 2015. From the first meeting, they can read it,"* said one teacher.

A teacher aide said of ineffective staff, *"They faceoff with the child and challenge, and the child ain't gonna back down, especially to a teacher."* I asked if that was linked to history and the teacher aide agreed. He suggested, *"Don't stand up and faceoff like a challenge and make a compromise, because they won't. It's one thing with black kids, they won't. But if you bring it across another way, instead of as a challenge or a, 'You must do this,' there's other ways of approaching it."*

A parent described an incident with a teacher who was sarcastic about their daughter who was accepted to a university. He reacted in a sarcastic way and laughed. The parent said, *"I actually took it to the attention of [the principal] and he said he's breaching the code of conduct. He should not bully a child and, yeah, I asked for mediation, which he failed to turn up at. That straight up aggravates a parent... and you can be told, 'Yeah, trust us, we'll do our job, and we'll see to it.' That's not good enough. We are people who like to deal with things face to face, Aboriginal people. And to have them present at a mediation is more than you'd ever know. And it's important because it gives parents a closure. When you're solving any matter."*

A different parent talked about a teacher who *"raised her voice a lot and [got] in the student's business".*

A teacher advised to not yell but use a *"firm speaking voice"*. This teacher also advised teachers not to *"dumb things down"*. We spoke about raising the standards for children and not just getting them to colour in.

Teachers were advised to retain a professional distance. An experienced teacher said we should not be *"getting too personal with the kids. It's very unprofessional in terms of wanting to be their friend. I've noticed that with some staff, more than teacher-student relationship."*

Teacher self-control was also respected. Several participants spoke about teachers who lost control of their emotions. *"The way she talks to them, like the ways she talks to the kids; a real angry way and an angry voice... angry words. She might go to this person, making like a horse noise like, 'brrrt,' you know."*

A father discussed teachers who don't stay in communities: *"Most of the white teachers that were there when, well they've had enough, mate, they just buy a plane ticket. Yeah mate, some of them just can't take it. You know, I suppose they're not strong, I don't know, when the going gets tough, mate, the tough don't get going I suppose. They just leave."*

This father spoke about persistence: *"Just being there for 'em, mate. Just being there and talking to them every day. And we tell all the teachers, and some of them tell us, too, mate; just keep hacking on. We'll get there."*

What teachers can do

These suggestions could easily apply to all teaching settings. Avoid dealing with behaviour when your emotions are escalated. Remain calm, as Christine Richmond recommended, save the passion for the content (Richmond, 2006). Follow through when needed. Avoid an 'I'm the boss' approach by earning respect and creating relationships, while maintaining a professional distance/persona. Avoid conflict and power struggles with students. Avoid sarcasm and put-downs. Be prepared to be persistent and resilient. That sounds like a pie-in-the-sky list of attributes, but they are ones that teachers will recognise.

Attitudes and strategies from theme 4

The attitudes in this theme are important because they relate to unconscious bias and an air of superiority. These are included in the lists below. An attitude of humility, a genuine caring heart and a willingness to learn will help teachers succeed with their Indigenous students. This is not simply about applying a strategy in a classroom, but the need for reflexive practice on the part of a teacher, to examine their beliefs, their approach and the results of their interactions with students. Read more about this and find resources at llewellynconsultancy.com.

Attitudes

✔ I make an effort to learn some Indigenous language/s.
✔ I work to have objective perceptions about Indigenous students and families.

Strategies

✔ I avoid sarcasm with my students.
✔ I avoid an 'I'm the boss' approach.
✔ I react calmly in a crisis.
✔ I apologise to students when needed.
✔ I reflect on my interactions with Indigenous students.
✔ I keep my word so students can learn to trust me.
✔ I verbally communicate high standards for my Indigenous students.

Reflection

I have so many good memories from teaching. I still connect with past students and hope I had some positive influence. Personally, I think that the willingness to reflect on interactions and improve has helped me as a teacher. Some of the qualities that have allowed me to teach for so long include: always being ready to learn and change; having a sense of humour; and genuinely caring for students.

I remember well the events in my teaching career where I got it wrong. I often used humour with students in the classroom (well, I thought I was funny and sometimes got a laugh!). At least it was entertainment of some kind. Relationships and humour were a strength and helped to make each day worthwhile. When I knew students well in a secondary context, we would be ribbing each other in a good-natured way.

On one occasion, I was sitting with a small group of students, and we were all 'having a go' at each other in a typically Australian way. A boy came into the group and obviously wanted to join in the fun. I directed a comment to him. He didn't take it well. He complained to a liaison officer and other students in the room had my back. The liaison officer and other students defended me to the boy, and I had an opportunity to apologise. The boy had had other things happening in his life and his resilience was low. That was an example of not knowing your student well enough, humour going sour and needing to repair a relationship. It was a lesson I did not forget.

Theme 5:
Positive relationships

" She can bother me, and it is because she cares."

(Lewthwaite & McMillan, 2010, p. 157)

Creating relationships was important in the literature I was reading. It stood out so much that while it is a teacher quality, it deserved a separate theme. But there were very few evidence-based suggestions for how to create those relationships. Relationships are critical for Australian Indigenous students. I asked participants how to create connections and their suggestions are included below. Friends have asked if these ideas could work for all students – yes, they may! My work on this could be the basis for similar studies with students of other cultures. In the TASSAIS Themes graphic on page 6, relationships sits inside teacher qualities.

Relationship before work

Something that non-Indigenous staff may not be aware of is that relationship may be needed *before* students will work for you. There was a new Physical Education teacher at the secondary school where I was working. She was having trouble with a class of girls. I suggested that she take some time to create relationships with the girls and make relationship a priority above the curriculum. She was surprised by my suggestion. It worked. Once the girls valued her, they worked on the curriculum with her.

What Indigenous participants said

As a teacher aide described it, *"If you've got no relationship with your students, they're not gonna want to listen to you. Like, they're not gonna do as they're told. So, you've got to come in there and like the same respect for them as they do, that you expect from them. Not go in there and think that you're better than them. You know what I mean? 'Cause they'll just say, 'Yeah, whatever...' 'Cause I've noticed that they give [supply teacher] curry. Because he thinks he knows, like he probably does, don't get me wrong. But you don't go in there dragging the kids down."*

Our discussion moved to power and control. The teacher aide mentioned a good male teacher who had 'control', *"[But he does it in a different way. He does it gently, setting boundaries without conflict.] Yeah, and they follow it. The majority of them follow it."* I suggested that this teacher take the time to get to know his students, meet their needs with food, learn some of the language and gain their respect, and she agreed.

One teacher expressed the link between respect, relationship and students being prepared to work. *"You are gaining respect... You are forming a relationship as well that, well, you gonna get them to learn then at the end of the day. You get them to learn, you get them to react and open up, whether it is a question on the board, or you want them to read a story, you know, things like that. So, by me sharing a piece of life or my heritage to them, they are able to go, 'Ah, you know, she's all not that bad. I'll do some work for her. She's not that bad. She's earned that.'"*

From another teacher, *"The mainstream teacher might, like if there's a problem, she'll want to know, 'Tell me, what's the problem?' Whereas with our kids, sometimes they won't. Sometimes they will, [snapped her fingers] this is the problem, other times, it's all these other things. They [are] showing that the problem is over here, that's the problem. And you only get to that after they think they could trust you."*

A school leader reinforced that relationships are paramount. *"I think the most important thing is, for teachers, and it takes a while to set up, but it's establishing relationships and maintaining those relationships through the good times and the hard times. I try and scaffold activities where teachers can build those relationships at the start of the year because it pays off later. So, relationship building with students and with families."*

A primary school student said, *"Because my mum, she loves me, and I love her, I don't want to lie to her because when you lie to someone, it's like you are making a bad decision."* For some students, the kind of relationship that students have with their teachers will determine their level of respect and cooperation.

What teachers can do

Accept that you may need to create relationships with students before students will want to work with you.

Connecting with students to create relationships

What Indigenous participants said

I asked the participants how a teacher could create relationships with their Indigenous students. A school leader responded, *"Investing in them. Taking the time, talking to the kids about the weekend, spending time with them outside the class, opening the classroom 10 minutes early for kids to come into a safe space; really important! Doing all those bonding activities at the start of the year – icebreakers, games, getting to know you, asking questions, being engaged, making the kids know that you care, that they're there – it's really important. If the kids have to go home or be suspended because of inappropriate behaviour, engaging with them as soon as they come back. So, it's not a hostile environment. Saying hello... My favourite time of the day is playground duty in the morning; really important, 'cause you get to say 'hello,' you get to say 'good morning.' You can check who's got lunch, you check who's going to [the] tuckshop, you know the kids that you need to check in with just to see how they're going... Kids just wanna know that they've established that relationship, so sometimes it is sharing what you do on a weekend, or sharing about your families or similar situations you've been in... It doesn't matter what information or the level of information you're providing, but just that you're engaging in that exchange of relationship. The kids are giving [teachers] part of themselves, you have to give them a part of you as well: a small story, telling about your favourite foods, talking about a book, just giving a little part of yourself."*

Or from a teacher, *"By just knowing what colour you like; their friends and parents; how many brothers and sisters they have. Build a personal relationship with them. Getting to know them. Show some interest in them. That's what I'm talking [about]. Otherwise, they'll just look at you as, 'Oh, there's the teacher. You don't know anything about me and stuff.' Get to know them, to be a bit easy on them and not to put them on the spot or anything like that. Don't notice hair, clothes, shoes. Don't say anything negative. Tell a positive comment."*

On a whole-school level, one senior secondary student noticed that, *"From day one, everybody said 'hello' to me. I don't even know them from a bar of soap. Every teacher! I'm like, I don't even know you. This is my first day!"*

A mother suggested, *"Taking an interest in the child as a person... listening at least. They don't have to react, but listen, they'll build a bond... There's some teachers who just have [a] knack I suppose with kids. That kids just instantly read their character, you know? ...There's some adults in education field that kids just feel safe with and that they can talk to."*

A primary school student said, *"They need to talk; they need to talk to you, talk to the students and get along with them... just try and be nice and kind to them."*

A senior boy said of one of his teachers, *"[He]'s like a jokable person, you know, he's a good teacher. He don't act like a teacher, he act like [a] friend in the classroom and that's what we would like. Teach us in your own, how you leave from work, how you act like, you know? You just talking to us like a friend. So, we bond to each [other], not just the teacher, you know?"*

That teacher respected students – but expected the same back. He prepared a PowerPoint presentation to show the students his family, pets, where he is from and his interests. The senior boy said, *"He tells them each week that [he] loves sport and that. I reckon it's had a bit of a difference, just knowing what your teacher's interests are, you know? Like, what he likes doing and stuff."*

This teacher and another would go and find new students in a boarding school and introduce themselves and invite them to come to class. Some staff would attend weekend sports when the boarders were playing.

A liaison officer said of a male teacher in a different school, *"Yeah, [he is] always welcoming, he gives them each the time they need. The door is always open, so it's never an issue. Especially the way you speak to them, having that relaxed flow of conversation; not being so uptight... Whether it is talking to them about culture or just in general, you know, something they've got that interest in, and you'll find that they work so much better if you do take those few minutes to have a little chat, setting the mood sort of thing."*

One teacher suggested to have an *"afternoon tea that invites their family members, especially if you are a new teacher and you're starting somewhere, like at a remote community at a new school".*

Further, a liaison officer advised, *"Well, you get to know the students. You spend a bit of time, you talk, you walk around your playground, get to know people. Get yourself out there. Don't hide in the staffroom or anything, so every time the kids see you... that's how they'll see you and that's how they'll treat you, too."*

From a teacher aide, *"Go on excursions. She [teacher] rewards them... she uses sleepovers. Our kids love sleepovers. [They bring sleeping bags] and they sleep here."*

Parents advised teachers to share some of themselves with the students. *"If he or she is a new [teacher], they could probably introduce themselves to the kids and say, 'I'm new, so please,' you know like... [Kids will learn how to] show the teachers... or respect them for who they are and for what they are doing. The teachers need to connect with the kids as well, like talking to them and telling them this and that,"* one mother said.

Another parent suggested, *"I think it's best to sit with the children, tell them a story, like what you've done, like what happened in the past, and I think the children will change and they'll see, I know. 'He's nice and he's caring for us,' the children will say."*

Staff emphasised connection. A liaison officer said of one teacher, *"She's really good at bonding. The kids love her."* Staff detailed ways to achieve that connection, through giving students time, through showing empathy and compassion.

One early years teacher *"talks to them, and the way she is with each child... I have seen her touch the kids and get down low"*. This was in a context where "'appropriate touch' (open body language) [is well received] as our children (and parents, as in this case) are masters at reading this" (Webber, 2024). Connection came from paying an interest in students' lives and getting to know them.

Also, being welcoming and *"having that relaxed flow of conversation; not being so uptight"*, according to a liaison officer. Ideas included spending time outside of school at sporting events or asking about the weekend. Some examples of making connections included celebrating birthdays and shouting a struggling student lunch on their birthday. Several staff mentioned telling a little of yourself; one teacher said, *"I usually share a lot with them about me for them [to] open up to me as well."*

Staff recommended *"checking in on them in the afternoon to see how they're going. Consistent care and reliability help, and just being there every day is... gold to them, you know... [one male teacher] hasn't had many sickies."* The consistent attendance of this teacher and the impact it had on his students was noticed by a teacher aide.

All of these suggestions will help to create relationships.

One particularly warm teacher spoke about her class: *"[They] read me like a book. Like, I had assembly this morning and they look at me and they are all smiling. This is what they say. I make 'em shame. Yeah, because they don't want me to do those kind of things [laughing]. 'Miss, why you have to do assembly?' Like that. 'Because it's my turn, all teachers have a go.' 'Yeah, but you make us shame.' 'No, stop it, you should be proud!'... They're like my children, you know... and I'm like the big mummy in their eyes, or the auntie. And we've got a special bond now, our little class."*

When you know students well, good-natured ribbing will flow, but it is important to recognise that the receiver will decide what is humour and what is hurtful. Students may not understand sarcasm but will read the tone of voice accurately.

What teachers can do

You can create relationships by sharing appropriate information about yourself, and spending time getting to know students and their families. Be approachable and confidential. Find an interest in common. Ask about their weekend or sporting events. Connect with students after a break or suspension. Most teachers do this for all students. For Indigenous students it may be paramount. The chaplain in one school where I worked had a 'bet' on a State of Origin football game with the upper primary school boys. His team lost and he had to run around the playground a few times to fulfil the conditions of the bet. The students loved it.

Respecting students

What Indigenous participants said

Parents spoke of respect and how to achieve it. As mentioned previously, a stranger automatically demanding respect is a colonial attitude and one that may not be familiar to the students. A school leader said, *"Well, if the teacher has that respect [for their students] when they go into that class, that respect will start flowing into that classroom. Like, say that teacher might say, 'What sort of day did you have?' or 'Can you better yourself to show me that?' or... 'I didn't mean to do what I done to you, but you need to stop what you're doing and listen to what I'm saying so that you know what you're doing.'"* Respect could also be shown by *"using the young person's name; saying it the right way",* and by believing students.

A liaison officer spoke about respect for students and avoiding idle or casual curiosity. *"I guess teachers ask them too many questions about their community and things like that, you know. I think enough is enough to them. They tell you bits about the community and about them. And that's where it stops. They don't want to tell you their whole life story because sometimes that's private. And they'll tell you things when they're ready."*

What teachers can do

In the reflection section for theme 2, I talked about how I have come to understand that the word 'respect' has different meaning in mainstream and Indigenous cultures. My understanding is that it means something like, "I will be safe in your hands." So, teachers can speak to students as people worthy of being treated well, particularly when using reactive strategies. They may be used to being on a more equal footing to adults than Western automatic authority in classrooms. So, valuing strengths and cultural knowledge, valuing differences in cultural capital and habitus is important.

Your cultural way is not the only way to see the world. It is vital that teachers value the soul and spirit of the students in their care. Most teachers already do this.

Listen to and believe students

What Indigenous participants said

Listening to students was important, an experienced teacher aide suggested to teachers. *"Listening is one of the best places to build bridges. Listen, understand where they're coming from, and you'll get the job done...*

because as soon as they know that, they understand that the teacher's listening, like nodding. Because most kid[s] want attention, you know? Once they get that good attention – not the bad one – you won't have issues in the classroom. And what I mean [by] bad one is that you don't listen to a kid, and he'll do something to get your attention and boy, if he do that!" This teacher aide saw the value of listening to students and the ways students would gain teacher attention if they could not get it easily.

One staff member complained that her daughter would not go to class because the teacher thought she was a liar. I don't remember every moment of my teaching career, but I do remember two occasions when I did not believe Indigenous students and I found out later that I was wrong about them. I thought I had not openly shown that disbelief, but the students would have known.

What teachers can do

Take the time to really listen to students. As a busy assistant principal, I probably rushed past opportunities to listen with culturally appropriate ears to what I was hearing. I related a story in the reflection for theme 1. When the Year 12 student told me that his family would be coming to dance at his formal, I accepted that, but in my Western way I wanted to know times, names, etc., and half doubted whether they would make it. When the dance performance happened, I was humbled by the ability and grace of his family as they celebrated his success. That was one occasion when I wish I had listened with my ears more open.

Some students will tell lies, but I learned to tentatively trust students until I had reason not to. I would ask them why they were out of class, for example. They would reply, "Mr... said we could be here"; I would say, "I will just check that with him." The kids would come back with "Gammon, Miss! Gammon", have a laugh and go back to class.

Attitudes and strategies from theme 5

The attitudes and strategies in the lists below are ways of measuring a teacher's commitment to students. They originated in the interviews, and were carried through the research project. If teachers have these attitudes and are frequently doing these things in the classroom, that is an indication that they have taken the time to create relationships with students. I suggest teachers consciously try to include some of these attitudes and strategies if they are not part of your current teaching style.

Attitudes

✔ I understand that students may need to make a relationship with me before they will want to work for me.

Strategies

✔ I act in a way that creates close relationships with Indigenous students.

✔ I let students know through verbal and non-verbal cues that I believe in them.

✔ I use my students' preferred names correctly when I address them.

✔ I am careful about creating attachments to one family or group of students because others may feel excluded.

✔ I understand that I must show respect to students in order to be able to expect respect from them.

Reflection

When I was asked for my purpose as a teacher, I would say that I was paid to teach Art, but my real purpose was to help teenagers. I helped them become who they needed to be. At times, teenagers needed me to hold a steady belief in them when they lost their belief in themselves. My metaphor was that I would hold that self-esteem for them gently in the palms of my cupped hands until they were ready to resume it themselves. I helped a young man one year who was discovering that he was gay, and there were other challenges in his life. He rarely attended school due to life events. When he did come, I showed him support and compassion. He failed Art that year, but I was able to help him as a teenager.

Theme 6:
Pedagogies that
support behaviour

"The classroom behaviour of students improved when a context was created in the classroom that was responsive to the culture of the learner."

Gillan (2008, p. 276), agreeing with Bishop (2003)

The main study associated with the Australian Research Council grant for my scholarship examined pedagogies for Indigenous children (Lewthwaite et al., 2016). For suggestions related to pedagogy for Indigenous students generally, read that study (and also Burgess et al., 2022; Lowe et al., 2021; Morrison et al., 2019; Yunkaporta, 2009). My focus here is pedagogical decisions directly related to behaviour.

Clear expectations and setting goals

What Indigenous participants said

Four students identified two ways they would like their teachers to be effective. The first was to explain the work clearly. *"She makes things easier, easier for those ones and the ones in case they need help,"* said a primary school girl.

One senior student suggested getting student attention by using Aboriginal Kriol or Torres Strait Creole. *"Like, my way, like the way I say... If you say 'Kriol', they get it just like that!"* So, they can *"catch it in their mind"*.

A staff member suggested *"making the time to go and speak with the child and ensuring that they are understanding the job. It's one thing to explain it to the class, but they still may not understand it unless you come and [give] them instructions visually."*

Another staff member said, *"Our kids learn by examples, so learn by doing... Because each child is different, so how they process the information that you give them is different, so you have to learn by example and show them exactly what you want. Then they understand. So, and then that's very important."*

A liaison officer suggested, *"Make sure the teacher explains it – what [it] is all about and then the kids can understand... If they don't understand, then [they] just ignore the teacher and go out... Sometimes the teacher doesn't explain it to the kids; that's why the kids come out and just wandering... 'cause the kids always tell me."*

Another suggestion was to make sure that children are listening, and for the teacher to use non-verbal communication to let them know they are waiting for some students.

A school leader discussed the need to be prepared and implement explicit teaching. *"Explicit teaching is really important, I think, for all children."*

Support staff described student behaviour in situations when students do not understand instructions and cannot access the help they need. *"Yeah, if a student doesn't know or understand their work, what they are working on, it could lead into aggressive behaviours, stuff like that which can erupt because even students themselves don't understand how to cope with their own feelings. Like they don't know what to do with them. So that's why they just push things and throw, 'cause they don't know how to control their own feelings,"* said a liaison officer.

One mother explained how a teacher spent extra time to help her daughter. *"Oh, he listened to her, and he explained things and she was a little bit, behind, not behind, but because she wasn't reading at home. They didn't have reading books, so she read them at school, and he used to get her to read at school, like some extra reading help."* This teacher used goal setting.

A teacher explained her processes. *"I personalise academic goals... I usually sit with them one-on-one. Or my teacher aide sits with them one-on-one... Before we fill in the paperwork, we usually get to know them first before anything. They write their three goals, but I said, one out of the lot that you really want to focus on, what is it, you know, it is attending class, little thing you know and that's what we try to work on."*

What teachers can do

Explicit teaching, using visual or experiential teaching were suggested. Teachers could also check that students understand the task in a non-shameful way and provide supports as needed. You probably think this suggestion is teaching 101. I have seen teachers who did not explain clearly, and it was important to the participants. Specific pedagogies for planning have been studied (Lewthwaite et al., 2016).

Helping students

At the end of phase 3 of the research, I added an item. This was that teachers help individual students in the classroom. I have found in my work that this is a crucial strategy. Some Indigenous students need help, and they work better when that help comes immediately.

What Indigenous participants said

One parent admitted the failing of most parents when it comes to Maths. *"You know, with Maths problems and whatever, hey, all Maths changed since we were at school. I can't even do it. Anyway, like some of our kids [are] lacking that literacy, numeracy part."*

In one school, 15 students is a large class, and those classes have their own teacher aide. This is a pedagogy that is a conscious choice to support student learning.

A priority was helping students who need it. Several support staff, for example, liaison officers and teacher aides, described how they, as students, and current students were more willing to work when they got the help they needed, acknowledging that it was hard for teachers to help all students. *"It's hard to give a lot of attention, too, like, if you put a kid in a classroom full of 20 students, and the teacher can only do so much as well,"* said a liaison officer.

It is difficult to help all students at once, but teacher aides and smaller class sizes make a difference. A teacher aide said, *"[Teachers] yelling doesn't get you anywhere. So, you really need to be relaxed, take the time. Yes, everyone understands that there's a deadline. There's only so much amount of time, but slowing it down, breaking it down for the children. Trying those steps, you know, explaining it one-on-one, putting them with someone else... I suppose instead of being the person that sits behind their desk all the time, moving around the children."*

A student advised, *"Know them [students] a lot, to know what they're up to, help them get to work, and if they're not as smart as the other one, work with them and help them a lot."*

A liaison officer said, *"If they [students] are struggling with their work and they don't want to say that they are, or it seems like they are not doing their work but they really can't just do it... they might get aggressive, like they might push the desk or something, and then I'll talk to them and they go, 'I don't know what I am doing.'"*

As part of her role of helping students, a teacher aide would, *"Go in the back room – we do have a back room – and to take their work with me, and we sit in the back room with them to do their work as well... One-on-one is excellent with the boys that I've got."*

An experienced teacher explained, *"Because I think, if they can't do the work, you have to sit next to them. They need an adult sitting next to them. They're not gonna say, 'I can't do that.' They just behave, walking around, not wanting to do this."*

What teachers can do

Providing individual help to students was a strategy that I added to the TASSAIS Themes list after the Rasch analysis (Bond et al., 2020), as during observations it became clear that students were less likely to be off task when they received the help they needed. In my experience that is crucial, but also difficult to achieve in current class sizes, and with staff ratios. I have seen teacher aides and teachers engaged with groups of students at a kidney-shaped desk to make assistance easier.

Trying to get to all students is draining on teachers in a large class. To reduce student anxiety caused by starting a task, we include strategies in behaviour plans, like ruling a margin and putting the date, then waiting for the teacher; turning a gel timer over and if the teacher hasn't come when the timer has finished, that is a mark against the teacher, leading to them wearing funny glasses or slippers. Students can also support each other, working in pairs or groups. Keep thinking creatively if this is an issue for your students.

Use storytelling and active learning

What Indigenous participants said

Traditionally, Elders taught using storytelling. A teacher aide said, *"Yeah, because most of the way they teach is pretty much like a story, but they tell a story about: 'This is what's the bad side of the story.' If you go down this track, then... and hear the other side of the story as well."*

A teacher recommended that active learning worked better than, *"Hav[ing] [students] sit there and have a person just talk, talk, talk, talk, talk."* Further, *"Yeah, definitely, that hands-on, just especially with the lower school. The problem with the Maths, you know, 'cause it is such a hands-on learning, it will eliminate certain behaviours straight away... [it] does eliminate a lot of issues because they're kept busy, and yeah, it's built for them [teacher] because our kids learn by doing, so you have to show them exactly what you want. Sometimes words are not the best thing. You have to show action."*

What teachers can do

Teachers could teach using the traditional method of storytelling to convey a message. One school leader related how she would use storytelling and discussion while hanging out the washing or gardening, rather than formally talking to her children, particularly her boys. I am a natural storyteller and find it useful when in front of adults and children. That quality saved my bacon one day. I ended up taking a fill-in lesson with no notice at all. I had seen a documentary about Pompeii the night before and shared that information as a story. Planning active learning rather than students sitting and listening will also help.

Questioning strategies

What Indigenous participants said

Cultural shame or being singled out may make students uncomfortable, so they may show reluctance to answer questions in front of others. A liaison officer said, *"Make them answer or make them like... They ask the* kid, 'What's the answer to this question?' Some kids would [feel shame], the black kids anyway. I might say the wrong thing. They might laugh at me."

What teachers can do

Implementing pedagogy that is aware of cultural shame is important (see theme 2). One effective teacher offered students ways out when asking a question. They could say "pass" so the teacher would ask someone else; "I'm still thinking" and the teacher would give more time; "come back to me" with another question; or "phone a friend", where the student chose a peer who could answer. Students adapted quickly to this way of avoiding 'shame' and supporting each other.

Repeated questioning of an individual student increases the likelihood that a child may feel increased shame. Also be aware that asking questions to which you already know the answer may be seen as a little crazy culturally. Asking too many questions may be seen as rude or intimidating.

Giving the big picture for curriculum

What Indigenous participants said

One school leader suggested using Indigenous learning styles, such as giving the big picture before you break a task into sections. *"I don't know whether this is like a learning style thing necessarily, because it links with the way stories and knowledge is passed on. But, going from [the] big picture, before you break it down... Western education seems to go step by step. You can have this little bit, and you can have that little bit. And you don't always know what the point of it is. But if you get the big picture, it's a bit like having a puzzle. This is the whole picture, and then we'll pull it apart and then we'll teach. So, I think that's a better way."*

Curriculum content was also raised by one teacher, saying she appreciated a mainstream school that provided some Indigenous content for all students and time for Indigenous students with an Indigenous staff member. Another experienced classroom teacher recommended that Indigenous students learn about other cultures, and not just their own culture.

What teachers can do

Teach about Indigenous content and cultures as well as other cultures. Show students the bigger picture of the content before breaking it into parts, as students may need to see where the pieces fit into the whole before they begin. So, if a class is learning a dance, for example, the teacher could show them the whole dance, before teaching them sections of it. This is another lesson that I learned. As a dance teacher in a Western style of dance, I would teach a section at a time, eventually creating the whole. I would also advise reading further about culturally responsive pedagogies (Lewthwaite et al., 2015; Lewthwaite et al., 2016; Morrison et al., 2019; Sam & McDowall, 2024; Yunkaporta, 2009; Yunkaporta & Kirby, 2011; Yunkaporta & McGinty, 2009).

Classroom decisions about choice, movement and group work

What Indigenous participants said

When talking about group work, one liaison officer suggested, *"You could maybe – if it's not individual work – pair them up with someone else that they can feed off."*

A teacher said, *"Now I'm just trying to change the teaching method to 'All right, let's all do this together!'"*

One teacher aide said she worked better in a group of Indigenous students when she was at school because, *"I guess, in a way, I didn't really feel ashamed answering questions. 'Cause if I was in class, like in Math, if I knew the answer, I would put my hand up. I felt really shamed at [mainstream school]."*

This comment was supported by a liaison officer who ran groups for Indigenous students in a mainstream school. Students may feel more comfortable in a group of their peers or working in pairs for activities.

They may also feel more comfortable outdoors. *"Because they function better on Country, too. You know, come outside because you're in a sterile classroom 24/7, and they feel like they are in prison."*

Movement was recommended by a primary school liaison officer. They said, *"[I] noticed here at [school], they make sure that kids have a fair bit of outside time as well, like they would break it off and have their classes, and between them they'll let them go out and have a bit of a run around or something and just burn a bit of energy off and then let them come back in."*

This kind of movement break and resettling was demonstrated by a teacher in phase 3 of my thesis. It was a regular routine for her class. One boy in classes I observed would go to the toilet three times in a session, not for the toilet, but for a movement and brain break.

A school leader suggested children be able to access a break when they feel overloaded. *"And maybe that's a learning style thing, I'm not sure, but I think that works really well... I think having spaces where, if the kids could become too complex for them, they can move away, and you have a quiet area in the classroom, and I don't think that matters whether you are six or you are 16 (or you are 60). So, they can actually go and stay safe in the classroom. So, having that structure set up, and having an environment stimulating enough, without, you know, being bored, or being too stimulated or something that could be sensory overload as well."*

Several participants mentioned students working towards free time as a reinforcement, negotiating time to choose their own activities and proactive movement breaks. A teacher said, *"The kids, they wanna arc up because, OK, they want their free time, they want this time, or iPad time, they want music time and things. So, I'm just saying we can do those things if we've done this or this or this. Or when you've done this [task], we can do this [free time]. You know, like going out with the crowd, having BBC [blow, breathe, cough (Hearing Australia, 2023)]. OK, when we finish this, we can go out. So, the longer you take to finish it, the less we have time out[side]. So, the kids work towards something."*

Blow, breathe, cough is a health initiative that includes 15 minutes of exercise followed by blowing your nose, which *"promotes clear ear canal"*.

What teachers can do

Teachers can offer paired or group work, arranging seating and groups for Maths and English. Choose groups carefully considering relationships and behaviours that would complement each other. Offer movement breaks, even if a frequent walk to the toilet is needed for some students. It will be a sensory break. Whole-class movement breaks have been used successfully in lessons I observed. Indoor and outdoor games provided the brain and body a movement break. Offer a quiet space to retreat to when needed; and sometimes students may need to sleep. Another practical suggestion is using a yarning circle, so that students are supported to participate verbally.

Strategies from theme 6

The strategies mentioned in the interviews and carried through the research are a starting point for adjusting learning to meet the learning styles of Indigenous students. Other research that has focused on this area specifically will have further suggestions. See the references mentioned in the previous section. The list below shares the strategies that emerged from the research for teachers to implement in their classrooms.

Strategies

- ✔ I provide opportunities for students to demonstrate their strengths.
- ✔ I use meaningful learning tasks for my students.
- ✔ I do not shame individual students by asking them repeated questions.
- ✔ I provide students with opportunities for group work.
- ✔ I use storytelling in the classroom.
- ✔ I allow students wait time if needed when I ask them a question.
- ✔ My classroom displays evidence of the cultures represented by the community.
- ✔ I include Indigenous role models in my teaching.
- ✔ I explain things clearly and in different ways so students will avoid any frustration of misunderstanding concepts.

Reflection

I have observed teachers using effective pedagogies such as frequent breaks, playing heads down, thumbs up to settle a class before work. That class became used to this settling activity. Humour, visuals, creating a family-like atmosphere all worked. In phase 3 of my study, I saw a very effective Art task that engaged all students. I related a story earlier where a teacher had shamed a girl, even though other students had tried to intervene. When I spoke to the teacher afterwards, she denied having shamed the student. I gave her the reading about 'shame' (Harkins, 1990), and I hope she reconsidered her habits. That lack of self-awareness on the part of this teacher is a large part of the problem teachers face, and the reason why self-report data in research is often different from observation data. I highly recommend observation data for teachers to reflect on their practice with a trusted observer. Find out more at llewellynconsultancy.com.

Theme 7:
Proactive behaviour
support strategies

"The employees outlined the difficulties that the young Noongar students faced when trying to adapt to an unfamiliar code of behaviour predicated upon White lines of authority that silently set limits for the sayable and doable."

(Gillan, 2008, p. 263)

Proactive strategies for behaviour support are those which are put in place to prevent inappropriate behaviours from happening. There are quite a number of these. At the end of this chapter, I talk about how my focus has become turning from reactive work to proactive work.

Remove barriers to learning

What Indigenous participants said

A parent mentioned troubles that children may face at home, and teachers may not be aware of why a child's behaviour is different from one day to the next. The teacher might wonder what is going on. One primary school leader described proactive support for students using a team approach: using a case management system to remove barriers to learning; using the counsellor; input from a behaviour specialist; a social-emotional learning person to teach social-emotional programs with each class; identification of a key adult to mentor the child; implementing an individual behaviour plan; contacting parents; accessing external agencies; access to health screening for sight and hearing; providing transport; and providing breakfast or a fruit break and emergency lunches if needed. This team also accesses external agencies for help, such as paediatricians, occupational therapists, speech therapists and psychologists. A parent suggested letting children sleep, if needed.

One school was equipped with a wellbeing centre that had a full-time nurse and Indigenous health worker, and visits from specialist teams of doctors, sexual health practitioners, a paediatrician and hearing and sight checks. This helped to reduce barriers to learning, which reduced off-task and inappropriate behaviours. The classrooms in one school were equipped with a hearing support system. One family was being supported by external agencies and needed a permanent address before students could be assessed. The school was working with external agencies to provide support. By reducing barriers to accessing education in practical ways, the school was helping to reduce inappropriate behaviour that stemmed from external circumstances.

What teachers can do

Teachers can tap into the ideas in the previous two paragraphs, for example, whole-school responses, administration support and wraparound support for the student, which have been successfully implemented by other schools. If teachers can see a barrier to learning, staff outside the classroom can help to identify the barrier and work to lessen its impact on student learning. Often, these initiatives require other specialty training (such as occupational therapists, behaviour specialists, paediatricians, psychologists, etc.); in this way, student support becomes a team response. A team working in tandem with a teacher can implement strategies and teaching to support wellbeing. This is where I spend my time. Whatever we can do to support student wellbeing and learning proactively will improve learning outcomes and a teacher's workload in the long run.

A group for Indigenous students

What Indigenous participants said

A staff member recommended that schools cater for Indigenous students by providing time with Indigenous staff. *"I like schools that have Indigenous focuses. One good school my daughter went to – and they don't even do it in [this town] – was they had an Indigenous teacher once every Friday, because they (in that place anyway), they had a handful of Indigenous kids. And I would always make sure that every Friday those kids got to spend time with that teacher, and they'd do things, like Aboriginal Art and talk about things... They celebrated things like NAIDOC day, they had people come in. ...[Her current school], they don't really embrace the Indigenous culture over there."*

A liaison staff member talked about her school days: *"When I went to school, we had [a liaison worker] and that was always making sure there is somebody in the school that is culturally appropriate that you feel you can come and sit down and have a chat to, I think that's very important.*

It doesn't matter where you go, Indigenous or non-Indigenous school, it's always good to have that somebody that, you know, I can just go and lay everything out and they would listen, and you felt comfortable. I always felt comfortable with her."

One school had a program for Indigenous students. *"If we have events on, like, for example, my [group] every Friday, they're encouraged to participate, even if they don't want to go there. Like, 'I know, it's OK, why don't you go along?' You know, they've got that interest there for the kids. So, that's another really helpful thing,"* said a liaison officer. Whether these students identified as Indigenous or not, she continued, *"They have that exposure because they don't always get that from home. Even though they're identifying home, parents don't know a lot about the culture as well. And just, you know, touch on those things... We're all the same, but being with those other Indigenous children who would have that understanding of what they've got as well... They come out of their shell. They're a lot more talkative, they'll stand up and dance! They've done that before, and they will be the quietest person in the classroom and they're just having that comfort. We've seen it... It's easy and relaxed, I try and make it so it's fun activities as well in there like, I'm not a hounding person as well. Some days I'm like, 'Let's get this done!' Sometimes we'll work in small groups. At the moment... the children are being given the opportunity to be leaders for our small kids... giving them that leadership, with their own kind, their Indigenous people."*

A proactive strategy in a mainstream school involved putting students in a setting with their peers because it created a *"safe place where they can really be themselves... [their] home life is similar to the person sitting beside them... they really come out of their shell. They're a lot more talkative. They will be the quietest person in the classroom [and in the group], they'll get up and dance,"* said a liaison officer.

Staff also recommended that schools provide an Indigenous liaison person or teacher aide with whom students could create a positive connection. These Indigenous staff related well with children due to the similarity of their own experiences and those of their children. These staff might present information differently, so students or parents could understand it.

What teachers can do

Teachers can request or create a safe place for Indigenous students to connect with others and adults from their cultures. It could be creating a tutoring afternoon that is a safe space, or a physical space where supports are offered. Liaison officers in schools will be able to help with suggestions and connections in the community. Your efforts in this space will be appreciated. I heard of a school where a non-Indigenous person was going to be employed as an Indigenous liaison support. This showed a lack of understanding on the part of the principal.

Use staff, community and family connections

What Indigenous participants said

Parents suggested the use of parent and community help. One mother sat in the prep class with her son until he had adjusted to the school environment. Another mother related a story where teenagers had tricked a naive staff member (not a teacher) new to the community by teaching him swear words in 'language'. Parents had to step in to educate the person who had been unwittingly insulting Elders around town. In this case, the students did not know, respect or trust the staff member and felt able to take advantage of his naivety.

Suggestions from staff included: not getting into a 'power struggle' (teacher); using the head of primary to back you up (school leader); firm, consistent strategies (three teachers and a teacher aide); and incentives (school leader, three teachers, two teacher aides and a liaison officer).

What teachers can do

This suggestion is unpacked in detail in theme 3. Connections with family will help teachers' cultural learning. It creates teamwork between family, school and external supports. Creating connections ahead of time will help to avoid the need for strategies after events.

Creating an environment and celebrating culture

What Indigenous participants said

Staff referred to the physical learning space making Indigenous students feel comfortable. A teacher said, *"Put up some posters. If you've got Indigenous children in your class, make them feel comfortable. Put up pictures of Cathy Freeman; put up stuff that these kids can identify with, you know, it is a safe learning environment where they feel comfortable. [Create a] comfortable learning environment; even with primary school kids, a big rug on the floor, but like a learning/yarning circle rug, with Aboriginal, Torres Strait designs on it. That's another thing, 'cause then they'll go sit on the rug."* In this school, the referral room had posters of Indigenous and non-Indigenous role models on the wall, demonstrating the classroom world view.

A parent praised a teacher who planned *"trips away where they do things like team building; activities like those sorts of things where they have no choice but to work together and stuff. And I think that does a lot of self-respect and respect for each other and working alongside each other, so they get along. Yeah, I found that beneficial."*

What teachers can do

One of the non-Indigenous teachers I observed in phase 3 of my study had many visuals across her classroom that were culturally welcoming. She also deliberately chose a task for students that was culturally relevant and personally exciting for students. This created an environment where students were more likely to engage in learning. I also see more flexible furniture and teaching spaces now than 10 years ago. These help to create a welcoming environment.

The benefit of teacher aides

What Indigenous participants said

Anyone working in schools knows the value of teacher aides. A parent related, *"Teacher aides should be brought back in all the schools, because... No teacher aide there, just one teacher and you got all these kids, you know, they just got no respect for the teacher sort of thing... Could be an Indigenous person; it could be a white person. It could be another support person within the classroom environment, so that like if one kid, he might go in and be in a real shitty mood, you know, that teacher aide – and that teacher might say, 'Oh, look, can you just take him outside, or take her outside, and just have a quick little thing to see what's going on?' And that's just told him that if he [is] having that break or if he's in that grumpy mood, you can find out what's wrong... so that if he's coming in and taking it out on everybody else and plus taking it out on the teacher, that sort of thing."*

What teachers can do

The Indigenous school involved in the research placed a teacher aide with each class. Many were Indigenous, and non-Indigenous staff were experienced in the context. This means the aide gets to know the students very well and is there for them. A deep trust relationship builds. This decision is not one that teachers make – it is up to leadership and budget priorities. Teachers can access Indigenous staff and community members to support students, or at least help to create a time and space where Indigenous students can gather and support each other. Teachers can also learn from Indigenous staff, as I have been lucky to do.

Respect for culture

What Indigenous participants said

An important piece of advice was giving kids space when they are going through 'sorry business'. This referred to the cultural protocols and ceremonies around funerals. A liaison person recommended giving students space to grieve if they need it. *"You have to be compassionate because they cope and deal with it in their own way. 'Cause if you're all in their face, they get, you know, sorrowful, in their face and everything. Sometimes they just need a bit of space, you gotta let them go, let them deal with it in their own way and then come to class. Just come to class and sit quiet there at the back, and talk when you are ready."*

What teachers can do

Teachers can recognise that other cultures value rituals, ceremony and family differently and respect those traditions. Teachers can then work to eliminate misunderstanding and judgement from their classrooms, and help students to catch up if they miss school time. There are many strengths in cultures different from our own, and learning about other cultures helps to expand our understanding. I found that my culture can learn about ways to process death and grief, and ways to care for the natural environment.

Understanding reasons for behaviour

What Indigenous participants said

Many conversations with staff concerned examining inappropriate behaviour for the cause or using a functional behaviour assessment to work out reasons for the behaviour, and structure the environment and interactions to remove barriers to learning. A teacher said, *"Usually, if there's something wrong with behaviour, it stems from something else, so you need to investigate that further, you know, one-on-one chat, what's going on? ...If you need further assistance with this matter, there are always people to turn to, for example, you can go down to [the wellbeing building]. Find a school counsellor, have a chat with them about it and tell them what your worries are. There's plenty [of] strategies within the school, also to help the child, you know, move along comfortably."*

Some possible reasons for behaviour suggested by staff were: not liking change, such as their usual teacher and teacher aide being away; students having experienced trauma; staff not understanding the impact of trauma; possible problems at home; a need for sleep; wanting to avoid the work; not understanding instructions; needing adult help and not getting it; being bored; having pride hurt through shame; fear of each other and not understanding each other's cultures; and stereotypes.

A liaison officer described what the students may be thinking: *"Like it's usually [at school] you ask for permission before you do something, you know? And I see other kids do it and I just stand up and do it, too. I totally forget that because I'm not at home anymore, I get into trouble for my behaviour, so I had to change. Because I see other people doing other stuff and then I just follow along."*

An experienced teacher aide had the wisdom to watch quietly in certain situations, to work out who was the 'head of the snake' – a metaphor meaning the starting point of the issue. He said, *"When I sit in the classroom, I usually just sit and if someone just [narks up] and I'm like, 'Oh, that, not like that.' You can tell that because I've been in it for a while, I know all the attitude and I know how they act in the classroom. And I wait, wait, wait, and then I see a kid and I was, 'Yeah, this was you!' And I would wait for a little bit and once he started talking, I was like, 'I was watching you the whole time. You're stirring everybody up in the classroom. I might as well go talk to the teacher and you're going to [reflection space]...' Because if you're sitting in a classroom where – for like a lesson or something – you can tell which kids are the attention seekers and which ones are the one that stirs up trouble and which one is the sly ones, you know?"* He also suggested that a supply teacher try to stick to the teacher's routine.

One liaison officer mentioned a strategy from the counsellor. Children who have experienced trauma may feel more comfortable at the back of the room, rather than have things happening out of sight behind them. They said, *"Staff need to change it up for each student instead of doing the same thing for the whole class."*

A school leader said, *"Knowing their history, and also knowing, like, other needs around their learning styles, which I think the teachers do a pretty good job of, a lot of the time. And I guess one thing that I've learned more about probably in the last 12 months, two years is the sensory needs. So, you know we talk about ODD [Oppositional Defiant Disorder], and we know ourselves that we fiddle with stuff, or we doodle or whatever when we're learning yeah, but actually recognising that that's now just a kid being naughty or annoying, that you know what do we put in place because there's quite a lot of simple things you can put in place that takes that away. And all of a sudden, that kid that couldn't sit still and was punching Jimmy beside him, whatever they were doing that was annoying, it is solved and it's calm… And then whenever there is a behaviour, looking at what is that behaviour really telling me, you know, if behaviour is a symptom of something, what is it?"*

A primary school teacher recalled student tiredness and restlessness: *"They're having stuff at home, then they come here, and they play up because, I don't know, they just don't feel comfortable anywhere I guess, and they want to be in control of their life."*

An experienced leader said, *"Also, think about pride, shame and hurt, and you know, what makes you…' cause often the stuff that makes a kid angry… The first thing that poor old teacher knows is that kid's just blown up and kicked the desk or sworn at somebody. But that could have been like an hour and a half coming up, so what else is actually happening around them, the young person?"*

A few of the participants suggested that when students trust staff, they will open up about what the issues are for them. One liaison officer said, *"If they build a good rapport with you over time, they will tell me. Like, if they are not switched on, they try to go other ways to make them look better?… Yeah, distract and be that class clown, and then you don't have to do the work… You know, some of them, if they don't understand something, that's their way out… I know one… he's Indigenous. He's really switched on. And I don't know if he carries on and plays up because he's bored? You know what I mean like, he knows the work. He can get it done. And if he does it, then he starts mucking up once he's done it. So, you know, there's two ways it could go."*

A student said that children use behaviour with a relief teacher, *"because they just want their teacher back because they don't like new teachers".*

A school leader explained how students might end up in fights. She was talking about how misunderstanding and the need to keep family safe contributed to fights: *"There's some silly stuff that's been happening and there's some people that haven't thought stuff through, but why is it that people are doing this? Because this is paranoid thinking, and everybody starts looking at this one and that one, and then everybody goes into that fight/flight thing so quickly. I don't know what the answer is with that. But that's part of the problem – that everybody goes into protection mode. I've got to keep myself safe, I've got to keep my family [safe], and sees everybody else as a threat. And all of a sudden, you've got a problem; where we should have just been able to sit down quietly and calmly and say, 'OK, she said this', but what really happened, 'Well, he said that', but what really happened?"* She went on to explain, *"Fear [comes] from not understanding each other's culture."*

What teachers can do

This is where I spend my working time, discussing behaviour with teachers and working out the motivations for behaviour, and adjusting environments and interactions accordingly. There are resources teachers can access to help them. Cultural liaison staff, counsellors, behaviour support teachers, experienced staff – all of these can help to unpack a behaviour and the reasons for it. Once we have an idea, we can reduce the frequency of behaviours that are not beneficial for the student and not appropriate for school.

I have worked on more than 300 plans and a handful have not worked for identifiable reasons. When students are respected and supported in the context, learning time can increase. A first step for teachers is to use curiosity (who, what, when, where, why patterns identified), rather than animosity (responding to behaviour in an emotional way).

Trauma background

What Indigenous participants said

One school leader directly referred to trauma: *"Kids also need to know how an adult is going to react to the different situations, and a history of trauma has told us that kids need to be able to predict what behaviour trusted adults are going to do, and how they are going to react."*

She explained how staff provide for students with a history of trauma. *"We have a case management system where we look at the needs of the kids... putting different strategies in and accessing different services for those high-end kids, so could be behaviour support with our behaviour specialist... or it could be additional work with the school counsellor. It could be identifying a key adult. It could be a behaviour management plan. It could be contacting the family. So, we have an array of strategies that we can use that can help with those high-needs children. It could be a referral to an external counselling service. I think it's really important to consider case by case, that there's not one answer that fits all, so, about looking at individual cases, the needs of the kids and what we can do to help. And what I think has helped most definitely is the team approach to those problems. So, it's working in a team environment with the parent, with the teacher, with the TA, with the school counsellor and with the head of primary and the liaison officer. And working as a team to figure out what works best. A team approach is definitely what works best."* If a child has experienced trauma, they may have triggers that set them off. *"It's like one of those panic buttons, you know? You push that kid and then he just explode[s]."*

What teachers can do

Learning about trauma and how trauma responses can manifest will help teachers to understand behaviours. One of the best books I have read is *The Boy Who Was Raised as a Dog* (Perry & Szalavitz, 2006). You can find further resources at llewellynconsultancy. com.

I worked with a learning support teacher in one school who had become resentful towards a student. The only data I could get from the school was her vitriolic emotional stories of his actions. I reorganised that data into patterns, enrolled the learning support teacher into several trainings we had on offer, and included the student's external psychologist in a case conference meeting. This woman was not a bad person or a bad teacher, she was exhausted and out of her depth. Teachers will reach down into the bootlaces to find the energy to keep helping students. With increased awareness and skills, this teacher found compassion and energy to turn her attitude around to support the student. You can find further resources on trauma at the above website.

Some function-based strategies we often use in plans to support students include:

- Understanding our own emotional/stress state and habits;
- Practising self-regulation so we can attune and co-regulate;
- Understanding the escalation-de-escalation cycle and its irregularity in students with complex trauma;
- The role of cortisol;
- Use of tone and body language;
- Offering choices;
- Not taking behaviour personally;
- Helping the student feel safe and reteaching expected behaviours;
- Identifying patterns and triggers;
- Teaching the student to identify their emotional state through their pulse rate;
- Inviting the student to join the group rather than pressure them; and
- Creating relationships.

Teach expectations

What Indigenous participants said

Parents recommended that teachers gently and explicitly teach new expectations. Another key point raised by parents was that teachers who relate to students could tell straight away if something was wrong and they knew which strategies might work for each child. *"It's actually knowing how to handle that kid, you know, suited to their needs, and you know if you know them. They should already know what works and how to talk to them by then, so it's easier for them [teachers] to deal with them [students],"* a mother said.

A teacher aide recommended, *"You set rules when they come in. This is how you behave. This is what they've got to do. Get your stuff, get ready."*

What teachers can do

Just that! Explicitly teach and model the expectations for behaviour. Teach routines. Teach social-emotional skills and how we treat each other to create a safe space in the classroom. Some students may need repeated teaching, demonstrations and practice to learn the expectations. Think about that teaching as laying down neurons to form a new brain pathway for decision-making. The student will use the previous inappropriate behaviour if it was successful until we create a strong neural pathway for a behaviour. When that is a strong alternative neural pathway, the student may be able to choose it. That means multiple reteaching events and reinforcement of the behaviour that is more appropriate for a learning environment, as well as responding differently, so inappropriate behaviour is less successful.

Whole-school strategies

What Indigenous participants said

Whole-school strategies for teaching expectations were raised by participants. These included arranging classes considering family dynamics, behaviour and relationships. A particular whole-school approach was mentioned several times, with one teacher saying, *"I think having the [school] way explicitly teaching for the whole college. So, it doesn't matter whatever class you're in, we can always quote and go back to this, is the [school] way."*

A school leader said, *"So, proactive strategies, explicitly, is of course the School-Wide Positive Behaviour Support [SWPBS/ PB4L] framework that we are currently using through KidsMatter."*

She went on to talk about teacher aides and their ability to engage students in the classroom. She said, *"I think you are talking about strategies that are whole school and proactive, like selected seating and fruit breaks, and mind breaks. One of the strategies we like to use is, if a child comes to you with a [whiteboard] marker from another classroom, they need that five minutes [to] cool down, so you kind of give the kid a small job to do and then they go back to try and counteract that behaviour. It's not about getting the kid into trouble. It's not about addressing behaviour. It's about giving them time to de-escalate before re-engaging in the classroom. It's just one small proactive strategy that can be used to de-escalate behaviour."*

What teachers can do

At the school level, evidence-based systems implemented with fidelity can create an environment that is conducive to appropriate behaviour (McIntosh, 2014; McIntosh et al., 2010). Teachers can look for evidence-based strategies that align with the whole-school strategies, for example (Blackley et al., 2021). Teachers can also be involved in those systems, so they have a say and influence whole-school decisions.

You can find references to whole-school approaches at llewellynconsultancy.com. I won't go into detail here, but I advise some examination of these processes as inappropriate school cultures can create difficulty for Indigenous students.

Social-emotional learning systems

What Indigenous participants said

One school consciously taught social-emotional learning skills to students. A teacher said, *"Having all those support programs, you know, like Bounce Back... I didn't think the value of that program we did bouncing back. We use it now. Like it's not even the activity, doing all the activity sheets. It's the discussion that we get out of it. It's the lessons that we get out of it. If we pull off something from YouTube, or something, but it's the discussion I find. You know, you can bounce back, and I think for our kids, they need to build resilience and if something happens, we can bounce back from that. Or they say, 'nobody's perfect,' I go, 'yes, you know.' And we all get little sayings from it."*

As well as Bounce Back (Noble, 2003), this teacher also mentioned Rock and Water (Gadaku Institute, 2002) and the Catastrophe Scale (The Bernard Group Pty Ltd, 2023) as useful resources for children.

Bounce Back was mentioned by another staff member, who said, *"They talk about creating these social stories and setting up expectations."*

A school leader agreed: *"We also run the Bounce Back program, which has worked really well this year. The teachers are enjoying it, the parents gonna enjoy, the students are engaged. It's a good conversational tool around behaviour and expectations and how to bounce back from different situations. That's definitely made a difference. The language being used around school at the same time... also Christian perspectives, implementing that into the curriculum is important than that food for the soul. 'Christian perspectives' teaches, I think, how to include Christianity in your life, and so, they're teaching you about the world you wanna see and support systems such as religion and that can kind of support as you go through... Bounce Back is a program that is designed to teach resilience in different situations. SWPBS explicitly teaches behaviour."*

What teachers can do

Get involved with choosing or designing social-emotional learning strategies for your school. These should be evidence-based, informed by neuroscience and implemented with fidelity. Examine which skills students need to develop and teach those. Consciously align any social-emotional learning programs with the morals and values of your setting. If there is no whole-school approach, find resources that will help you to develop lessons and activities to teach culturally appropriate skills to your students.

A visual monitoring system

Importantly, in contrast to previous research where Gillan (2008) found that students resented a public display of behaviour records, my research suggested differently. The reason could be that Gillan's work was conducted in a mainstream school, while mine included one primary school that had 100% Indigenous students at the time, so Indigenous students in the classes were surrounded by their peers. In this school, students and staff spoke positively about behaviour records being visible on the wall of the classroom as a way of teaching and encouraging behaviour that was appropriate for school. Students did not resent the system being used and staff relied on it, particularly at the beginning of the year, to teach expectations.

What Indigenous participants said

Several staff referred to a visual system for monitoring and motivating students. Several primary school teachers and teacher aides spoke about a chart or scale on the wall and moving names up and down, or daily points counted towards something at the end of the term so that students could monitor their own progress. The visual in-class behaviour scales ranged from pegs on a card to ClassDojo points (ClassDojo, 2011) and visual escalating steps to time out with a buddy teacher.

One teacher commented, *"I think visual helps because they can see what tracks them, you know, keeping track on how well they are sailing along throughout the day."*

Initially, reinforcements included external reinforcements, like iPad time, free time, afternoon tea, sleepovers, class parties and excursions. One experienced teacher detailed how this process was inclusive, supportive and avoided shame in her class. *"I don't like to exclude children, but if I feel you haven't earned it, I will. So, I don't like exclusion and the less exclusive activities I do, the better. 'Cause I like it to be inclusive... If I see you've made an effort and you're nearly there, I will let you go. But I'm not even using that reward chart now. 'Cause, you know, as a class I think you deserve to go, everybody's trying. It's not perfect but... I needed [the reinforcement chart] in first and second term. I needed to aim for something. They'd go there and count that and then if we seen something good, if my kids seen something good, we'd put it on there. And they directly saw it, you know. And they needed it that first and second term. And if there was a person who wasn't reaching up, I'd go, 'Is there something that you can do, you know, to get some more points?' And you give them their own little target to get to the point where they're up; the goal is bigger for the other kids but, you know, they have smaller goals. So, we push them."*

This teacher used the chart graduating from extrinsic to intrinsic reinforcements to move students towards behaviour that was more appropriate for learning in her classroom.

What teachers can do

In secondary school, one or two teachers used steps or warnings on the board leading to a referral room. This referral room actively problem-solved behaviour with students and staff, rather than being a minding service. There is a debate in the literature about extrinsic reinforcements. Please note that the definition of a reinforcer is that it will increase the likelihood of a target behaviour reoccurring. While adults may think a reward is suitable, students may not. At one school, staff found visual reinforcements useful. One way to view reinforcements is to see them on a continuum from extrinsic to intrinsic (Deckers, 1996).

At another school, students were not used to being inside in a learning environment. We used a food reinforcer for the groups whose attendance was over a certain percentage. It worked and attendance increased. In that case, intrinsic reinforcements could not start until students were actually with the teacher in the classroom where relationships could be established, and success experienced. Teachers could also find new students outside of lesson time to create relationships. If your class contains predominantly non-Indigenous students, be careful about any public shaming. There are ways to reinforce groups of students, rather than individuals, which takes away individual shaming (Riffel, 2024). Be aware of your particular context and the potential for shaming students around behaviour.

Be aware of the function of student behaviour. This awareness helps staff to avoid reinforcing behaviour that is inappropriate for the social setting and learning. This can also help staff structure natural consequences rather than relying on punishments to decrease the frequency of a behaviour. Teaching a new behaviour that is productive in the setting will help the student meet their needs. I offer training in functional behaviour assessment.

Classroom strategies

What Indigenous participants said

Proactive suggestions given by staff for individual classrooms included: checking that things were OK after lunch and settling any problems (teacher aide); giving students some quiet space when needed (school leader, teacher); and meeting sensory needs because there are *"quite a lot of simple things you can put in place that takes that [sensory need] away"* (school leader). Also, knowing the student's history, and how they learn best (school leader); finding out the problem and what happened before they came to school or class (three teachers); and letting students have time out and they'll come around slowly (teacher, two liaison officers).

Staff also suggested: having well-established routines through being consistent (two teachers); using a seating plan (primary school leader); arranging classes carefully (primary school leader); reminding students when transitions are coming (secondary school leader); planned breaks (primary school leader); distraction (primary school leader); giving kids space (liaison officer, teacher aide, teacher, secondary school leader); selective attending in some situations (secondary school leader, teacher aide); and using some Creole/Kriol (teacher).

A teacher said, *"Language, say things in language. Like the Creole, break it down to Creole. If you're a bit cranky, talk in Creole. Language, yeah it works, because they sort of look at me and... 'How did she know my language?' You know what I mean... And they respond to me."* The teacher also suggested, *"Having a goal, and reminding them of the goal; showing progress visually."*

Also, a secondary school leader recommended visually and practically supporting students through school routines, timetables and transitions.

One teacher recommended stepping into a situation early while problems were still small if it was looking like a negative situation might happen with the kids. In a longer-term sense, a Torres Strait Islander liaison person used the metaphor, *"Grandpa always say... when you have a kid, you get straight to that kid when he smoke, before it comes to an adult. So, like bamboo, green bamboo."*

Several teachers recounted how students helped to motivate each other to reach that goal in learning or behaviour. Students also celebrate each other's successes (teacher, teacher aide). Several other staff recalled whole-school practical proactive strategies like frequent breaks and a classroom seating plan (school leader, two teachers).

Also, a school leader recommended teaching pro-social skills: *"[A specialist] will do social-emotional programs with each class, targeting different things like, in the lower grades we do protective behaviours... It's really important 'cause... no one else teaches those skills about how to solve conflict... and I think that, as we continued through the journey of the last two years, the number of critical incidents in [this part of the school] is diminishing and it's falling. And we're getting kids talking about their feelings and talking about the behaviours instead of fighting. ...because if kids are talking, they are using the language, they're talking about the strategies. I could have done this, this or this, but I chose to do this, and I made this choice. And that's a good thing."*

Other strategies included making sure the teacher aides were aware and consistent with the teacher, and making sure all students are focused and listening before you start (teacher). An experienced teacher suggested counting down from five to one to get students focused. Some secondary staff suggested keeping student phones at the front of the room (teacher, two teacher aides). Staff recommended reminding students about the expectations and the goal they are working towards (two teachers, teacher aide), whether that be a personal achievement or an external reinforcement. In one school, all categories of staff also referred to the whole-school proactive program they were involved in, which included proactive teaching expected behaviours and social skills.

What teachers can do

If you are not reading all the statements by the Indigenous participants, go back and read the suggestions in this section.

Strategies from theme 7

In my experience, any time spent on proactive strategies saves reactive work. Reactive work is much less pleasant. It is pleasing to see so many proactive strategies emerge from the interviews and carry through the research project. These are listed below.

Strategies

✔ I offer students choices, so they have some autonomy in the classroom.

✔ I teach students to respect and care for each other.

✔ I explicitly teach my Indigenous students behaviours I would like them to use at school.

✔ I structure activities for students to build relationships with each other.

✔ I model for my students the behaviours I would like to see in my classroom.

✔ I use liaison staff/nurses/guidance counsellors to help me understand what is happening in regard to student behaviour.

✔ I use less intrusive behaviour support strategies like refocus on the learning to address inappropriate behaviour.

✔ I access school programs that teach conflict-resolution skills to students.

✔ I seek to address barriers to learning arising from sensory needs, disability, tiredness, hearing and hunger.

✔ I commend students in an appropriate way for showing behaviours that are suitable for school.

✔ I use visual reminders in the classroom to support student behaviour.

✔ I cue students to the behaviours required for transitions from one activity to the next.

✔ I engage with a student after he/she has returned from time out or suspension.

✔ I use 'I' messages in conversations with students about behaviour.

✔ I have well-established routines.

✔ I involve students in deciding classroom behaviour expectations.

✔ I explain to students that behaviours encouraged at school might be different from their home culture.

✔ I implement boundaries to avoid behaviours, for example, I will move a student.

✔ When I suspect or know that students have experienced trauma, I adjust my behaviour strategies.

✔ I respond to problems between students quickly, so the problems don't become bigger.

✔ I teach my students about the importance of our classroom operating on the principles of equitable conduct.

✔ When the class is working on a task, I help individuals and groups.

✔ I try to look for the reason for inappropriate behaviour.

Reflection

When I train staff in functional behaviour assessment, I always ask them to consider how much of their role is reactive and how much is proactive. Some staff are shocked when they work it out, particularly year coordinators and deputies. Proactive work is much more effective and more pleasant to do. It helps to meet the needs of students and encourage them to participate and learn in classrooms.

I use the metaphor of mopping up the water or turning off the tap. When I was an assistant principal in a secondary school, I would take a list of things to do and not even get to glance at it. I was too busy each day mopping up the water after various behaviour incidents. When I moved into a behaviour education officer role, I was trained in proactive work. Now that that is my soapbox and my focus, let's use what we know to do as much proactive work with behaviour as we can, so that there is less reactive work to do at the end of the day. I now have data from schools, staff and individual children to prove that proactive work can change behaviour.

TURNING OFF THE TAP

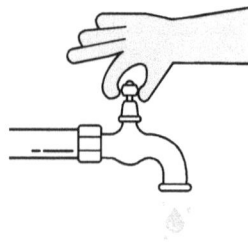

Mopping up the water?
Turn off the tap!

Llewellyn Proactive Metaphor

Theme 8: Reactive behaviour support strategies

"Noongar students essentially code-switch in response to the demands of the White constructed discipline policy. If teachers are to respond in a culturally sensitive manner when disciplining Noongar students then it will be necessary for them to perform their own epitome of code-switching by culturally differentiating the sanction applied for the misdemeanour."

(Gillan, 2008, p. 268)

This theme is important for teachers in Australia because responding to behaviour that is inappropriate for the context, or interrupts learning, is a necessary part of our work, and it is often poorly supported by research and training. There was no previous Australian research with evidence carried out focusing on reactive strategies. There were strategies suggested in advice literature, but these did not have empirical proof of their efficacy. These TASSAIS strategies have research evidence, and I will be working towards further proof of their efficacy. Before you read this section, please keep in mind your awareness of public 'shaming' for positive (appropriate for a school context) or negative (inappropriate for a school context) reasons. Your awareness of shaming should be carried into this theme.

The manner of staff

What Indigenous participants said

The calm persona, attitude and approach of the teacher in a reactive situation is important to avoid an 'I'm the boss' approach mentioned previously in teacher qualities. A liaison officer said, *"Instead of as a challenge or a 'You must do this!', there's other ways of approaching it. There's more subtle ways instead of standing there like chest out, finger out. You go over and put your hand on his back [and say], 'Come on, brother. What are you doing?' You've got to talk to them... It's more the body language than anything. You can challenge them in a good way, but don't do it in a bad way, in that tone. They hear it and they'll react. You've got to do it in [a] good way but not angrily, because they'll sense it. Yes, and then they will get defensive, then their shield will come up and 'F... you!' and all that. It's how you say things and how you do things. And it's all got to do with your body language and your tone... Well, it's an intimidating way. If someone's pointing at you, talking in, a demeaning tone... and there's other people around, you don't want to be shamed – [by] the kid. [If the teacher comes] chest out, demeaning look, demeaning tone and authoritarian, the child will put a shield up and he will call you every name under the sun and walk away from you. He doesn't want to talk to you because you're angry. And to avoid shame because he doesn't like you shaming him in front of his friends."*

Also mentioned several times was sitting next to students, as opposed to opposite them or standing above them.

A teacher said, *"I never raise my voice whenever I get cranky at them. You know what I mean. It's just certain ones, you know."*

A parent said that at home, in the community, the teachers have lots of patience: *"They have the tolerance, yeah. And they just walk up to the kids and talk to them, and if they can't control them [or] the situation, they just get one of the school attendance officers in a bus and go down and pick the parents up and bring them up [to school]."*

A liaison officer suggested to take control of a situation: *"If someone tells them what to do, they'll just go 'No!,' 'cause they want to be in control. Then there is that conflict and they run away. So, yeah, it's a matter of sitting down, I think. I have noticed here that a lot [of children] like, if you fight back with them, they'll only fight with you more and just take off. But if you sit down with them on their level, they will usually open up."* He said that the parents support teachers and Indigenous officers in the community and work together to help the kids.

A school leader recommended those in authority, *"talk calmly with the kids, sometimes ignore behaviour that is not helpful for the young person or the situation. Commend kids that they're doing the right things. Go alongside and, you know, sometimes, just quietly insisting, rather than reprimanding, even their behaviour [as opposed to criticising the young person], not talking to them about behaviour in front of everybody where it will shame them, like catching up with them later maybe, but just making sure that it's done quietly, it's done low level. Using the young person's name, saying it in the right way, you know... A lot of it's about fear of each other and not understanding each other's culture or language and stereotypes."*

When responding to behaviour, a school leader suggested talking about the behaviour and not the child. *"Sitting down beside the students at their level, talking in a calm voice, not using angry words, not direct body language."* This was also expressed directly by a parent and a liaison officer.

An experienced teacher suggested offering the child several options in a reactive conversation.

Staff stressed the need to intervene early, to remain calm. Teachers should give students space and choices to cooperate, so they can save face to avoid shame. Staff also mentioned consistency: *"Consistency, I suppose you'd call it, in the way that you react and deal with things with a sense of fairness."* And *"Consistency is a huge factor as well, I believe, in everything. Whether it's behavioural, classroom rewards, you name it."*

When responding to low-level behaviours, staff suggested that, *"Kids are gonna have bad days, you know. And not every day is gonna be a good day. Kids come with their own issues and problems and whatever... You gonna give them a bit of room to breathe, you know? But sometimes, if I see some of my students are having a really bad time, have something with it, whether it's sorry business, I let them have time out. They can catch up on their work, I let them have time out because at the moment, they just can't do the work in their state. Or I sit down to help them read. Or tell them to get a pillow and lay down for a little bit. And then [they are] so much better after, you know, instead of pushing, pushing, pushing, pushing. Just focus on resting for a little bit and then we'll get back into it."*

This is reminiscent of Maslow's Hierarchy of Needs – we can't engage higher-order thinking when we need sleep or when we feel unsafe or emotionally escalated.

What teachers can do

Many good suggestions came from the interviews and are included above. Finding out what really happened is a good first step. Research showed that Indigenous students were often not interviewed after an incident and before a suspension (Gillan, 2008). Arguing with students is a waste of time. Take-up time is useful (Rogers, 2002); giving the student a chance to cooperate. Deciding a time to talk later could help. Distraction may work. This could be the most opportune reteaching moment. Reteaching an expectation will help to build the brain pathway to make that behaviour a choice. This is a good time to employ patience. I have drawn on the student's relationships with others by asking for their advice. Collecting data, in hard copy or even in your mind, may be useful to look for patterns. If a consequence is needed, and if it would be useful to change behaviour, Blackley (2022) researched relevant teacher decision-making.

When dealing with escalated inappropriate behaviours after they have happened, be aware of your own emotional state and how that might impact on the situation. Keep your brain calm or arrange a tap-out code for others to relieve you if you can't recognise your own emotional state. In one training, we used, "There is a phone call for you at the office that you need to take now." Also recognise whether the student is calm, and if not, and if possible, allow them time to regulate their emotions.

When you are talking with students, be aware of your language register (keep it simple), your tone (calm and not condescending) and your body language (open and not threatening). If you can, sit beside a student and relate a similar situation or story. Avoid an 'I'm the boss' attitude as it may not be received well. Keep Maslow's Hierarchy of Needs in your mind.

Does the student need safety/movement/sleep/food/drink, etc.? Be aware of possible trauma responses. Does the student need a feeling of control over decisions? If so, allow them as much decision-making power through choices that still fit with the school requirements. Be aware of the 'shame' factor and deal with things as privately as possible. Remember to breathe, which will send oxygen to your brain. Approaching calmly and rationally will help. Be aware of nagging and using too many words at this time. The skills I learned to use in crisis situations have helped me when in public.

Avoiding 'shame'

What Indigenous participants said

Shame was frequently mentioned during staff interviews; avoiding shaming a child was very important to them. It was a 'big deal'. Several staff recommended coming quietly later to talk to a student when they were calm, rather than causing pain in front of everybody. A liaison officer suggested, *"Do it quietly, subtle, you know, without others knowing about it, I think. Especially when they're old... they will be shamed."*

A school leader said, *"We want them to acknowledge their behaviour and be responsible and find a way to move on from their behaviour as opposed to shaming them because of it. And I think an audience would shame people."*

Further, *"Singling them out, that's another huge thing, where they don't need to be singled out. If you've given them choices, and of course limited choices at that. Rather than single them out or yell at them, talk to them individually, quietly, or pull them aside – that's a huge one as well,"* said a teacher.

While a liaison officer said, *"Talking to the kids in front of other kids, they get pretty shame[d], then that makes them walk out."*

Parents also recommended that staff should avoid shaming students after an event. Staff should talk respectfully one-on-one with the student without an audience. Yelling was discouraged. One mother said, *"Talk to them in a proper manner way, not like yell at them in the class and say, 'Oh, you've done this wrong and that.' Talk to them like... Don't get them up and point at them and start accusing them of things, you know, just talk to them like you talk to a proper person, having a conversation beside you. If you talk good ways, they'll talk back to you good ways. If you try to talk and show them up, they get that real, 'Oh, this teacher really don't care about us.' If they talk to them in a disrespectful way, well then, the kids are gonna say, 'We'll talk back the same way to them.' But if she talks to them like, you know, proper conversation that don't show them up in front of all their friends, because they're gonna have that sort of macho situation."*

A teacher said, *"If you come and approach children, the pain happens in front of everybody, so I'm finding now, 'cause I got older kids, if you come later to them quietly, you'll get the reasons why... Sometimes I'll make a general announcement... so this person doesn't feel like I'm just picking [on them] and other times I bring the child aside and say, 'This is what you've done, this can't happen, this is the reason why.'"*

What teachers can do

This is a very real cultural difference that non-Indigenous folk need to hold in their awareness. The cultural shyness and wish to not stand out can mean that while we think we are rewarding students, we could be shaming them and decreasing the likelihood of a certain behaviour happening again. Shaming students could harm the relationship with them, and students would be less likely to cooperate. Some students may accept public praise, some may not. Group praise and group reinforcers may work better.

Talk to students without an audience, allow them ways to save face. Don't see a conversation as a power struggle, but as a cooperative effort. Students may be responsive to a reminder of their responsibilities in the family or the family of the classroom. Calmly offer a choice that allows students to save face and decide on a course of action to repair any harm caused. Most will understand their part in an event. If they don't, then some individual teachings may be needed at another time.

Family involvement

What Indigenous participants said

Accessing family help to support student behaviour was a strong recommendation by staff and parents in this theme. A primary school leader recommended early and frequent communication. Parents may have information about the issue which the student may not have been able to communicate to the school.

One father who worked in a different school said teachers at his school call the Indigenous staff to help with behaviour, not to make it their responsibility, but to help increase staff understanding. He described how the school Indigenous workers were included. The staff had separate meetings one week (Indigenous and non-Indigenous), then whole-staff meetings the next. If an issue arose, the Indigenous staff would *"run it to the principal and the principal runs it to the teachers"*. Another said they involve Elders to support parents. One strategy that worked in one of the target schools, as well as a community school, was for a family member to come to the school and be in the classroom for a time.

In one class the teacher offered a boy to have attendance as a personal goal. He would be working towards earning a sports team shirt as an external reinforcement goal. He succeeded. His mother came to visit the school and all she wanted was the best for her boys. *"She came to class a few times with [her son]. He was very respectful towards her, and [made] sure she was comfortable in the classroom. And with her presence in the classroom, he worked beautifully. He worked beautifully beforehand, but it's just that this little boy came to class and just sat and enjoyed learning. And mum, she was helpful. And it was, you needed that. You need a mummy around, too. It was great. They [families] need to see what school their kid is going to, and to see how well they're taken care of. So, having families here is beautiful. I don't know any other school that does that."*

A boarding school found ways other than face to face to involve parents. As one parent related, *"Sometimes they do teleconference. If they can't get the kids into the [conference] room and they teleconference from there... Well, they'll sit and listen, and they'll probably think about it. You know, they're probably thinking to themselves, 'Maybe I won't do that bad thing. I'll listen and do the good thing.' Maybe make the teachers proud or the house parents proud, or the parents. And if they do that, then they'll be on the right path. [Family] talk to them about problems, listen to them. Listen to their problems. You know, like talking to them in a good way and making sure that they behave in class or at the dorms. And the teachers see those kids when they get tired in class, sleeping on the table, and the principal, when they see that child sleeping, they know that they're [having] problems at home, so they get the Elders to a meeting and talk to parents about their kids, and making sure they're going to school; having clean clothes and that."*

One staff member was also a parent and auntie. She said, *"I sit with them when [teachers are] growling at them. [Teachers] contacted me, 'Aunty [Sharon], the girls weren't in the class.' 'Cause I came over. That's why I sit with them."*

This was also suggested by another parent. She said, *"He did have problems in the school, so myself and my mother, mother of my grandson, went into the school. Talking to him, to the teacher. Like, mostly, we were talking to my grandson that he needs to listen to the teacher. He needs to learn, and now he forgot all about it and how he's at boarding school right now."* In her community, the teacher would go outside to sit with the child, *"to calm them down, best go and sit with them".*

One senior student described her reaction if her parents were notified about her inappropriate behaviour. *"If the parents is [involved in] discipline… If you called my parents, oh, my God! I would be in trouble. My mum would be like, 'Oh, my God, I didn't teach you this.'"*

My personal understanding has grown to include that students will often respect family more than school staff, so connecting with family will increase respect for teachers.

Another parent said, *"I've found, because I've worked in the schools for years, I've found that when you say something like, 'OK, I will contact your parent and have your parent come in now,' they really snap out of it really quickly."*

Another recommendation was, *"If they don't listen to you, go to the Elders. Because there, they will really stop and listen to the Elders."*

Not all parents will support school decisions. Many of us have experienced unhappy families, but getting to know the family as advised in theme 3 and using liaison officers will help. A liaison officer said that *"most parents do care"* if they are contacted. Some children don't care if the school wants to call their parents. Some *"run back to class [saying], 'I'll be good, I'll be good.'"*

What teachers can do

Connecting with families early has been recommended in previous themes. When I tell Indigenous people I meet what this book will be about, this is the strategy they recommend most frequently. Involving families will help the student to see that school and home are working together – it will help staff to understand the situation better. It will show the family you are aiming to support their child. There may be a cultural solution to an issue that you are not aware of. Theme 3 recommends contacting families early, to establish relationships before an intervention is needed. Work with the family to find solutions.

Early intervention

What Indigenous participants said

A teacher aide explained that, in her role, she will intervene early if she sees someone is upset. *"The kids go out and have time, then I go out... when somebody's carrying on, they [the class] can get back to work. I let them have their time, and we watch them and then I go OK, I'll go ask them, 'Do you wanna talk about it, or even wanna come back in?' We sort it out. I don't like them [to sort it out] straight away, I like to do it later. I don't like to bring them back straight, you know."*

Two boys fought in her classroom, and she kept them separated until the situation was resolved. She encouraged both boys to have their say and then apologise to each other. She offers them options to fix the problems. *"My kids, I've learned now, you gotta give them options. Instead of saying, 'You have to do this,' it's, 'OK, you wanna do this?' or 'You gonna do this?'"* She also suggested bringing yourself back from a battle with them, withdrawing from any argument they want to have. *"I won't get into that battle 'cause they want you sometimes to get you into that battle."* They may need to vent their emotions.

A teacher explained how she used early intervention. *"I think [teachers should use] proximity, I think people get that wrong. They see that even things are happening over there. I get up and move into it. 'Cause if the kids are ready to chuck or tip [desk], I'm there. So, I've had a case, yeah. Now like teachers say, 'Oh they've tipped up this [desk in that teacher's class, for example],' I go, 'Well, I'm there before it happens... I'm there ready to shift them...' I don't get up into their face, but I get into that, what's happening, 'cause I like to do that gesture. I think it's their body signs, you know. You get agitated, faces get a bit steamed up, you know. It's getting tense. Yeah, so I like to go in, close in. So, we have hardly any cases of kids tipping up [desks] 'cause I like to think I get in there, and let them go outside."*

What teachers can do

Teachers can attempt to understand a situation and help to resolve it early. Situations left to fester can grow to a much larger problem. Watch the body language of students. Try to work out what is at the base of the issue. Give students time to vent and listen. Students may be able to resolve a situation by themselves, but monitor them to make sure they are supported.

Other strategies

What Indigenous participants said

Ideas from parents included: to talk to the kids and ask their problems; give them time to think about what you have said; listen to both sides of the story; and deal with things quickly. A teacher said, *"If you see something out of the corner of your eye, don't let it go. Just say, 'Hang on, I seen that!' and call the two students and say, 'What are we going to do to sort this out?'"*

Secondary school students appreciated teachers making a reasonable request rather than being reprimanded, and preferred the teacher who had a private conversation with them rather than one who used public shaming. When a teacher talks *"loud and strong"*, kids do not like it and would *"go off and swear back"*. Instead, what worked was *"telling them what to do and make them feel good and talk – like gentle and talks quietly, not like in rough ways and stuff".*

Another suggestion from a student was to address the whole class rather than individuals, *"[so, we're talking to everybody] so they can make them want to come, too"*, said a senior girl. An example of this strategy would be to evaluate an activity or behaviour with the whole group, rather than pinpointing individuals. Applying a consequence to the whole class rather than individuals only serves to alienate more students, but a gentle conversation could be undertaken with the class or group.

Staff offered detailed suggestions for reactive strategies that would be more culturally appropriate than targeting students, yelling at them or embarrassing them in front of others. All teaching staff suggested several reactive strategies that were successful. They detailed some low-level responses. One teacher told a story of a girl who was trying to access adult attention, and said she was *"ignoring [low-level behaviours] at times when that seemed to work".*

A school leader said, *"Sometimes ignore behaviour that is not helpful for the young person or the situation."* They also suggested, *"Planned ignoring. I like the idea of planned silence. Give them that extra time to be able to take things in. Especially our ESL [English as a second language] learners."*

Parallel praise was also recommended. This means to cue the student who may be off task, for example, by recognising on-task behaviour in another student.

Staff mentioned the effectiveness of non-verbals, and a teacher gave *"physical proximity"* as an example.

Students knew one experienced teacher's expressions; the teacher said, *"I just have to stand there and look at someone and I have that look of, 'I'm waiting for you.'"*

Staff also mentioned using a time-out space, going for a walk, counting and buddy class as consequences as part of the school system, but also that for some individuals, certain things did not work. In these cases, the school implemented an individual plan for behaviour.

Teachers should also watch for students bullying or teasing each other, sometimes because of cultural differences. In conflict resolution between children, it was suggested that staff might use storytelling to negotiate a resolution. A staff member who was also a relation of the children recommended that teachers *"take the child to a quiet place and sit with them and have a chat"*. Yelling at a child would make a child angry. Growling (rousing at) them in front of others is no good; sitting beside them is a good idea. Non-verbal strategies were also recommended.

A school leader mentioned several reactive strategies. *"De-escalate early on, separate the kids out. Not doing that whole reprimand thing [blaming the whole group]. Giving space and allowing them to recover, talking about the behaviour and not the child. I think sometimes you can see some teacher they go back to, you know, some of those 'I' messages – 'I felt'... And then some you can see with other kids that isn't gonna work. So, they actually talk forward, rather than going back to... So, it's interesting because not the same strategy will work for everybody either, and I think that's about them knowing the young person as well. Using simple language... you can see that the young person is not in a space where they can reason, you know, not trying to use that time, that reasoning time, just let it be quiet, letting that space be there. And then later on they're coming back, and talking around. Where the incident was and trying to put stuff back together."*

A different school leader talked about taking a student away for a while because the teacher may have had a stressful day. *"If you [take the student back] too soon, then it is just going to continue to escalate, it's like, the teacher gonna get stressed; if the teacher's stressed, the child's gonna get stressed, problems gonna get bigger without being fixed."*

A liaison officer advised that she would sit with a child who needed a break when a teacher was worried that he would run away. *"No, they are fine, they're not going to run away, right? No, they're not. They just need some chillout time, and then because they hear me say that, then they don't run away and then they'll just sit there and then I'll walk up and I'll go, 'Look! You're not in trouble with me and I don't know the story yet and I just want you to chill out. Take a deep breath and when you're ready, you can like talk to me about it. If you want.' And then I'll wait for them a bit and then usually they've just come around. But because I'm not coming for them and I'm just sitting there and waiting. Some of these kids go through so much trauma, they're probably used to being hit or something happening to them, you know, and if that's what they're used to, then somebody do that at school to them as well. They're having two upset environments."*

She advised the teacher not to hold the child. If he had experienced trauma... *"Nobody wants to be held, it doesn't matter how old you are."* She said it could be due to teacher frustration.

A time out was suggested, allowing a child to sit outside for a couple of minutes, *"to refocus. 'Sort yourself out, get a drink, go to the toilet. Come back in when you're ready and we can start again...' It works well for boys and girls."*

One secondary school put in place a referral room where problem-solving took place. Students could self-refer for a time out; talk things over with the young man and sort out what was happening. Staff and students could talk things over when people have calmed down.

A parent suggested, rather than suspending a child or sending them home, that *"A teacher could sit down and have a (eye-level) real conversation with the kids. You know, like come to school. Like, if you have an issue at home, don't bring it to school 'cause you put everybody else down in the class. And because you're upset, somebody say something, you're gonna take it out on them and it's gonna turn [into a] thing, because she's trying to teach them something. They're not want to listen because this other kid's got a shitty mood… Make it like a teacher-student relationship sort of thing so you don't have to talk to them… If you talk to them and find [out] about them, you know and take them to one side and you could just have a little… friendly conversation with them about what they want to do with life and whatever. Just put them to one side, or just take 'em outside and have a talk to them. Excuse himself and go out and then let the kid come back and it was a different story. And everyone else is here to learn, and if you don't want to be here now, say now and we can arrange for you to be somewhere else."*

An effective strategy that staff also utilised was to access help from outside of the classroom from the nurse and counsellors. One teacher said, *"There's plenty of strategies within the school, also to help the child, you know, move along comfortably."*

One school leader spoke about her own boys and culturally appropriate ways of dealing with behaviour. *"When there's been [the] need to have a chat, their uncles have taken them. You wouldn't do that. So that you are doing something. Whether that's gardening, fishing [or] hanging clothes on the line, but it's physically doing something, talking, you know. Especially teenagers, especially teenage boys, and also thinking about the shame because for a young man, if you're starting to talk to them, they know they've done right or wrong by that stage. But with pride, it can be hard to admit that you're wrong, and it can be hard to bring that out. So, it's about, sometimes kinda ignoring what's happened so that you don't talk directly to it, but you talk around what needs to happen. So, if you talk to what exactly happened; as in 'you did this, you then, da da da,' then it builds on the shame, then they get angry, then they're not listening. So, if you're talking around, maybe like a story, you might say, 'Look, I don't care what happened, I don't know what happened, but I'm thinking sometimes, it looks like this or looks like that, and what we need to get to is things looking like this or that.' And then, that lets them recover from whatever went wrong, and they can go back and like, whether it was a fight with their sister, whether they did something wrong in the house. But breaking something or doing something the wrong way that they should know, but they can set it right without you telling them to set it right. If that makes sense. 'Cause saving face for boys is very important and I don't know if it's 'cause the older boys, I notice, their dad is Aboriginal/Torres Strait Islander. And the middle one is very much like his father, and that pride stuff is very important. And he's very different, I noticed, in a way that they would respond."*

Structuring a restorative chat in this way was recommended as a culturally appropriate way to deal with behaviour, particularly with teenage boys.

Staff agreed that following through with consequences was important, as one liaison officer pointed out, *"because [if] there's no consequence, they know they can do anything".*

One example of following through was related by a secondary school teacher. *"I used to give her three chances, now I am down to two. And one of the things I do with her... 'cause we had to take baby steps with her."* The teacher gives her warnings, then she goes to the withdrawal room. The teacher has not had to reach that stage yet. If the girl knocked a chair over, and *"chucked a little tantrum, I said, 'Are you gonna pick that up? 'Cause I am not picking it up after you.' And I left it at that, which eventually she picked it up."*

I asked if she got angry or stayed calm, and the teacher responded, *"I did use a growling tone, or you know, a really firm tone, teacher-like voice type when, not getting up them really bad [not rousing really seriously] I would just say, 'Are you gonna pick that up?'"* She has not had to go to extreme lengths with her class. She raised her voice a couple of times and they *"usually fall back in; they come right down, and they behave well".*

I asked what would happen if a non-Indigenous teacher like me walked in and yelled at them. She responded, *"They would probably not behave for you at all for that whole session or walk straight out and that would be a negative impact and image on you. [It would be scarring] to them."* As an unfamiliar non-Indigenous teacher, I would need to take a different approach.

What teachers can do

This section is another one where you would be best to read the suggestions made by participants. There are so many ideas here and they are expressed well.

Practices to avoid

What Indigenous participants said

Parents complained about the way behaviour issues had been handled in the past. One parent identified that, *"They blame the kid, and they want to get them suspended and things like that 'cause when I've worked the problem out, they could sit down and talk to the kids. The easy way out for everyone is to just send them home. My kid's got anger management, but they send him home straight away."*

A staff member suggested not to nag. *"Constant nagging. Just picking and picking and nagging. It's not necessarily teachers. Some teacher aides tend to nag to students; we need to stop and see that... What works better that I use, is giving them instructions and saying it in a really polite manner. Because some kids don't take demands lightly. So, you would ask them to pick up after themselves and leave it at that. Walk away. But keep an eye on whether they are [doing] that. Following through [with] instructions."*

Another parent was angry that her children were suspended in a case of mistaken identity. *"They've been mistaken identity with my children and there were consequences that came with it and punishment, and in the end, they decided to suspend both my children because they looked similar and the wrong thing that they did, like they almost locked them in the office together for about two to three hours without contacting me, making no contact. And one of my daughters had a phone and she in-boxed me on Facebook and I went in there and I wasn't a happy parent. And the outcome was I disenrolled my children on the spot."*

Research has uncovered that Indigenous children were often not heard, and more likely to be suspended than non-Indigenous children. Listening to all parties is important. Staff suggested that, *"If the teacher talks to the wrong student that didn't do anything, you start stirring – boiling the kettle up and then obviously they're going to flip and you're going to have another naughty kid in the classroom."*

This situation was documented in phase 3 of my study. A school leader recommended, *"Not every two situations [are] exactly the same, but the kids need to see that when there is a problem, you talk to both parties. You investigate both sides. You see what each person was responsible for and what they need to kind of acknowledge and sometimes apologise for. So, just seeing the whole picture and not just, 'I get it all the time, I had a kid sent up [to] the office last week.' I had a relief teacher in place, and [the boy] had gotten in trouble for apparently scratching someone's back with a lead pencil... as the story was told to me, it may have happened a little bit differently, but the relief teacher had yelled [at] him that he had done it, without actually asking what happened. 'Cause the [back] got scratched, [she] didn't know who it was 'cause it was behind [her]. So, it took me about 15 minutes to figure out the kid should not be blamed for it [as] he wasn't actually responsible, his friend was. So, I have to have that kind of conversation, but the behaviour escalated. 'Cause he wasn't treated with respect, I think, or a sense of fairness. Actually investigate the situation."*

This school leader saw her role as intervening when the teacher was inside the problem in the classroom. *"They have 20 kids; they have had a stressful day. They have six different things going on with four different people. They don't typically get it wrong, but she [school leader] can step in to de-escalate the child and try to re-engage them in the classroom. In front of children, as much as you can, you support your teaching staff, but while at the same time making sure the kid is looked after, and things are dealt with appropriately."*

Two parents pointed out that their children had been treated differently from 'white' students in the past and that Indigenous students should be treated the same as non-Indigenous students. The mother said, *"Just because you're Indigenous doesn't mean the incident report shouldn't be filed, or [parents] shouldn't be informed. Like every other school, the parent is supposed to be informed and that's where [there is the] biggest downfall. A lot of regulations slide when it comes to [certain independent schools]. Like everything gets really slack. And if they were to work in a mainstream school, they... [are] contacting the parents [and] incident report[s] are part of everyday procedures. There's been a lot of times at [this school] where things that happened I've never even been told about because it was an in-house [issue], so I should have been told of the incident... And because my children come home and told me, I've been more angry with that because I'm not being told by the school direct. And the school doesn't inform me of the incident, you know. Maybe they had not intentions of informing me or intended to inform me a couple of days later, but that's not good enough because it's an Indigenous school. I expect to be informed on the day of the incident... The situation's only changed with me because I've [gone] in and rattle[d] the school up. And I think that's why they probably recommended my name to you, 'cause I go in there and tell them this is what should be done. This is how you should do it."*

This parent was also not happy that her daughters were treated differently from the boarders as they have to be sent home when suspended. Her children were suspended for two weeks at the end of the term and missed out on submitting assessments. *"So I've asked and pushed for them to be reassessed due to this [being] beyond their control and they still failed it anyways. And I found that was to be unfair and it was not looked into. And I'm all about education with my children."*

Another parent was not happy when her child walked out of the school and the staff did not call her to let her know. She said the school should have called to let her know where he was as it was the school's responsibility. *"If he walks out of my yard and catches that bus, you guys [school] are responsible for that kid on the bus. When he gets to that school. Yous are responsible, and when he comes home, soon as he steps off that bus and into my yard, I'm responsible for him. Till then, you guys are responsible."*

In another situation, a female liaison officer had family on the phone with the principal and told the children in front of the principal, *"Make sure you talk to your teachers, and we don't want [to] hear the kids can talk to us and tell us through crying."*

It was suggested by staff that mistakes included restraining students and keeping them in the classroom or letting an issue fester if there was an ongoing situation. Coming in from the playground there may be issues that need to be solved. A liaison officer said a mistake could be not listening carefully to find out what happened, then yelling at students without knowing the real situation. If a teacher was to guess what the problem was and just picked a kid to yell at, then you'll have another naughty kid in the classroom.

A school leader advised teachers not to be, *"Screaming at kids, not letting go [of] stuff, even just talking too much sometimes, when the kids aren't in a space where they're gonna listen. Confusing one kid for another, to really knowing the kids well enough. When the kids come in late, instead of letting them go sit in their seat and quietly set stuff out for them, drawing attention to the fact they're late, then the kid's getting angry, and so instead of letting go of it here, they keep going with it as well, 'Why're you getting upset? I'm the one who should be upset!' So, really not thinking about the kid's perspective. You know, it's disrupted their day 'cause their kid's come in late... Not being prepared, or, kids are at the class, waiting for the teacher, before the teacher gets there, you know, and then not having the stuff [lesson] ready."*

What teachers can do

Teachers should avoid blaming the wrong student, misidentifying a student or rushing in to yell without understanding the full story. Listen to both parties and don't skip processes just because students are Indigenous. Consider the child's perspective and don't get involved in picking on students or nagging them. You may think these things don't happen in teaching, but obviously they happened as the participants were speaking from experience. It would pay for teachers to avoid similar events.

Strategies from theme 8

Strategies suggested by interview participants have been reduced to the list below. You may take further ideas from rereading the words of the participant Indigenous staff, students and families.

Strategies

- ✔ If I need to speak to a student about behaviour, I take them away from other students so that the talk is private.
- ✔ I listen to both parties after an incident.
- ✔ When a student is upset, I use simple language when talking to them.
- ✔ I sit beside students to talk to them after an incident.
- ✔ After an incident I don't talk directly about what happened, but instead talk around it, for example, "sometimes these things happen and what needs to happen is this".
- ✔ After an event I offer the student options for help to set things right again rather than punish them.
- ✔ I selectively ignore some minor inappropriate behaviours.
- ✔ I follow through with consequences after an incident.

Reflection

As teachers, we don't get it right 100% of the time, but we can learn from our experiences. I advise teachers to reflect using this process:

1. What happened?
2. Later on, what really happened? You may see things differently after a break.
3. What did I do?
4. Next time, will I do the same thing or choose a different response? I may have done the best I can and would do it again; or I can learn from an event and try another response.

Evidence for the attitudes and strategies, working to developing an ethic of practice

Evidence to support the TASSAIS attitudes and strategies is available in my thesis and will be in an academic book I aim to write. I will be continuing research, looking for further evidence to support the efficacy of the TASSAIS work.

The figure opposite shows the progression of the research to gain evidence for the effectiveness of the TASSAIS strategies. The first oval is the TASSAIS Themes that came from the literature review. The second oval is a collection of the items from the interview participants; the first draft of the list. The third oval is the survey instrument, which listed the attitudes and strategies as items in the survey. The next one is the TASSAIS list refined. This was manipulated into an observation tool which was used to measure the relationship between the TASSAIS items and student on task time. In the next phase I will work with teachers to help them develop their practice and collect evidence of improvement. The end product will be a TASSAIS Ethic of Practice.

I was also able to find evidence to support my hypothesis that each teacher had a different style, that is, that each teacher had strengths and preferred strategies that they used more than others. (This evidence is in chapter 6 of my thesis.) For example, one teacher chose an engaging and effective task; one used her strengths of facial expression, humour and relationships; and one used effective pedagogy strategies. Not all teachers need to do the same thing. We know that teachers have a preferred style, and the evidence supported my hypothesis. You will develop your personal style as you find the attitudes and strategies that suit you.

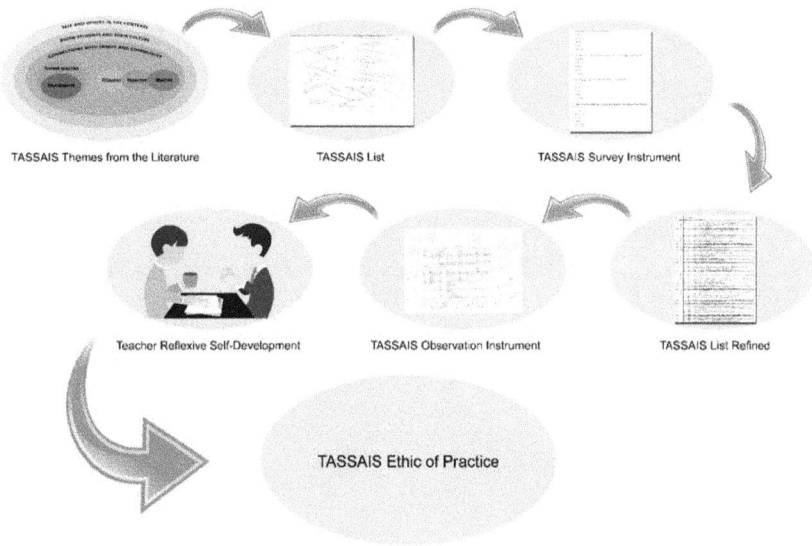

TASSAIS Themes from the Literature

TASSAIS List

TASSAIS Survey Instrument

Teacher Reflexive Self-Development

TASSAIS Observation Instrument

TASSAIS List Refined

TASSAIS Ethic of Practice

Conclusion

Indigenous students receive a disproportionate number of suspensions and exclusions. My literature review identified that there was a gap in research on this topic, particularly evidence-based reactive strategies. The TASSAIS attitudes and strategies come from Indigenous people and were tested for their utility in phase 3. Ideally, if culturally responsive pedagogy and cultural awareness are implemented, there would be little need for them.

Unfortunately, there is often cultural misunderstanding in behaviour events (Partington et al., 2001), and that could be one of the reasons. With an understanding of who you are in the context, an awareness of your own cultural background (field), your skills (cultural capital) and an understanding of the hidden curriculum in schools (habitus) (Dalal, 2016), you are more likely to understand your place in the context of school. Getting to know your students and their backgrounds, habitus and strengths, while increasing your understanding and strategies, will improve your ability to support student behaviour.

In my work life, I help teachers increase their understanding of student behaviour and watch as they reach down to their bootlaces to find more energy, patience and time for these students. It was increased understanding that was needed. I hope my work can prepare non-Indigenous teachers with understanding and strategies as they teach Indigenous students.

References

Atkinson, J. (2002a). *Trauma trails, recreating song lines: The transgenerational effects of trauma in Indigenous Australia.* Spinifex Press.

Atkinson, J. (2002b). Voices in the Wilderness: Restoring Justice to Traumatised Peoples. *University of New South Wales Law Journal, 25*(1), 233–241.

Bernstein, B. (1970). Education cannot compensate for society. *New Society 26,* 344–347.

Bishop, R. (2003). Changing Power Relations in Education: *Kaupapa Māori* messages for 'mainstream' education in Aotearoa/New Zealand. *Comparative Education, 39*(2), 221–238. doi: 10.1080/0305006032000082443

Blackley, C. (2022). *Teacher decision-making: the fulcrum of a productive teaching and learning environment.* (Doctor of Philosophy), University of Southern Queensland. Retrieved from https://research.usq.edu.au/download/d7100f08722457c049f3d ca9e90e93eb878f1286a8748b7daf0c48f5106f725b/7475535/Thesis%202021%20 WITH%20UPDATED%20PUBLICATION.pdf

Blackley, C., Redmond, P., & Peel, K. (2021). Teacher decision-making in the classroom: The influence of cognitive load and teacher affect. *Journal of Education for Teaching, 47*(4), 1–14. doi: 10.1080/02607476.2021.1902748

Bond, T., Yan, Z., & Heene, M. (2020). *Applying the Rasch Model: Fundamental Measurement in the Human Sciences.* Routledge.

Burgess, C., Bishop, M., & Lowe, K. (2022). Decolonising Indigenous education: The case for cultural mentoring in supporting Indigenous knowledge reproduction. *Discourse: Studies in the Cultural Politics of Education, 43*(1), 1–14. doi: 10.1080/01596306.2020.1774513

ClassDojo. (2011). Where classrooms become communities. Retrieved 10 December 2024, from www.classdojo.com

Dalal, J. (2016). Pierre Bourdieu: The Sociologist of Education. *Contemporary Education Dialogue, 13*(2), 231–250. doi: 10.1177/0973184916640406

Deckers, L. (1996). *Motivation: Biological, Psychological, and Environmental.* Allyn and Bacon.

Gadaku Institute. (2002). Rock and Water. Retrieved 2 November 2023, from www.rockandwater.com.au/about-rock-and-water

Gillan, K. (2008). *Technologies of Power: Discipline of Aboriginal Students in Primary School.* (Doctoral dissertation), University of Western Australia.

Harkins, J. (1990). Shame and shyness in the Aboriginal classroom: A case for 'practical semantics'. *Australian Journal of Linguistics, 10*(2), 293–306. doi: 10.1080/07268609008599445

Hearing Australia. (2023). Blow Breathe Cough. Retrieved 2 November 2023, from www.hearing.com.au/blow-breathe-cough

Houston, S. (2002). Reflecting on Habitus, Field and Capital: Towards a Culturally Sensitive Social Work. *Journal of Social Work, 2*(2), 149–167. doi: 10.1177/146801730200200203

Lewthwaite, B., Boon, H.J., Webber, T., & Laffin, G. (2016). *What Aboriginal and Torres Strait Islander students in North Queensland say about effective teaching practices: Measuring cultural competence* (conference paper). Paper presented at the American Educational Research Association Annual Meeting, Washington, DC.

Lewthwaite, B., & McMillan, B. (2010). "She can bother me, and that's because she cares": What Inuit students say about teaching and their learning. *Canadian Journal of Education, 33*(1), 140–176.

Lewthwaite, B., Osborne, B., Lloyd, N., Boon, H.J., Llewellyn, L., Webber, T., Laffin, G., Harrison, M., Day, C., Kemp, C., & Wills, J. (2015). Seeking a Pedagogy of Difference: What Aboriginal Students and Their Parents in North Queensland Say About Teaching and Their Learning. *Australian Journal of Teacher Education, 40*(5), 132–159. doi: 10.14221/ajte.2015v40n5.8

Llewellyn, L. (2023). TASSAIS Survey, available from llewellynconsultancy.com

Lowe, K., Skrebneva, I., Burgess, C., Harrison, N., & Vass, G. (2021). Towards an Australian model of culturally nourishing schooling. *Journal of Curriculum Studies, 53*(4), 467–481. doi: 10.1080/00220272.2020.1764111

McIntosh, K., Craft, C.B., Moniz, C.A., Golby, R., & Steinwand-Deschambeault, T. (2013). Implementing School-Wide Positive Behaviour Support to better meet the needs of Indigenous students. *Canadian Journal of School Psychology, 29*(3), 21.

McIntosh, K., Filter, K.J., Bennett, J.L., Ryan, C., & Sugai, G. (2010). Principles of Sustainable Prevention: Designing Scale-Up of School-Wide Positive Behavior Support to Promote Durable Systems. *Psychology in the Schools, 47*(1), 5–21.

Malin, M., Campbell, K., & Agius, L. (1996). Raising children in the Nunga-Aboriginal way. *Family Matters, 43*, 43–47.

Marzano, R.J. (2007). *The Art and Science of Teaching: A Comprehensive Framework for Effective Instruction*. Association for Supervision and Curriculum Development.

Miller, W. (2014). *Swimming the River*. [YouTube video] Retrieved 5 December 2024, from www.youtube.com/watch?v=0P9FRacTji0

Morrison, A., Rigney, L.-I., Hattam, R., & Diplock, A. (2019). *Toward an Australian culturally responsive pedagogy: A narrative review of the literature*. University of South Australia.

Nakata, M. (2007). *the* cultural interface. *The Australian Journal of Indigenous Education, 36*(S1), 7–14. www.cambridge.org/core/journals/australian-journal-of-indigenous-education/article/cultural-interface/B8321A596C2BFF62FA6B81E7F214BC38

Noble, T. (2003). *Bounce Back!* Pearson Education Australia.

Partington, G., Waugh, R., & Forrest, S. (2001). Interpretations of classroom discipline practices by teachers and Indigenous students in a Western Australian secondary school. *Education Research and Perspectives, 28*(2), 51–82. doi: 10.3316/ielapa.200210237

Perry, B.D., & Szalavitz, M. (2006). *The Boy Who Was Raised as a Dog: And Other Stories from a Child Psychiatrist's Notebook*. Basic Books.

Richmond, C. (2006). *Next generation behaviour management*. Ashton Scholastic Seminar notes. Ashton Scholastic.

Riffel, L. (2024). Behavior Doctor. Retrieved 24 April 2024, from www.behaviordoctor.org

Rogers, B. (2002). *Classroom Behaviour: A Practical Guide to Effective Teaching, Behaviour Management and Colleague Support*. Paul Chapman.

Rogers, C., & Freiberg, H.J. (1994). *Freedom to Learn* (3rd ed.). Merrill.

Sam, T., & McDowall, A. (2024). "Smooth seas never made a skilled sailor": Indigenous students' academic buoyancy and the locale of the learner. *The Australian Journal of Indigenous Education, 53*(1).

TASSAIS Survey. (2023). Available from www.surveymonkey.com/summary/ymusf6cvbZyTM3NcQL30IR4_2Bda6E0LgA17gstZbvkVY_3D?ut_source=lihp

The Bernard Group Pty Ltd. (2023). You Can Do It! Education. Retrieved 3 November 2023, from www.youcandoiteducation.com.au/product/poster-catastrophe-scale

Webber, T. (2024). Via personal communication, 5 September 2024.

Yunkaporta, T. (2009). *Aboriginal pedagogies at the cultural interface.* (Professional Doctorate Doctoral dissertation), James Cook University, Townsville.

Yunkaporta, T., & Kirby, M. (2011). Yarning up Indigenous pedagogies: A dialogue about eight Aboriginal ways of learning. In Purdie, N., Milgate, G., & Bell, H.R. (Eds.), *Two Way Teaching and Learning* (pp. 205–213): ACER Press.

Yunkaporta, T., & McGinty, S. (2009). Reclaiming Aboriginal knowledge at the cultural interface. *The Australian Educational Researcher, 36*(2), 55–72. doi: 10.1007/BF03216899

Acknowledgements

As a visually creative person, my metaphor for the research was a complicated jigsaw puzzle. The process to investigate, refine and communicate this information was a long one. At times I could have put the jigsaw down and walked away, but an internal drive to improve the experiences of Indigenous children and their teachers would not let me fail. The topic itself demanded that I finish it. This is my opportunity to thank those who gave support and allowed the jigsaw to be completed.

My humble appreciation goes to all of the participants in interviews and focus groups who cannot be named. With generosity of spirit, your expertise provided the pieces of the jigsaw.

Since we first met, Gerry believed in the potential of my work. I thank Helen for suggesting that I apply for the scholarship, and Brian for guidance starting the process. Then Professor Nakata and Kerrie for supporting me to finish the jigsaw, and Trevor, without whom pieces would have been missing.

I am grateful for emotional support from my children, family, and wider social network, particularly Chris and Kelly. At times it felt like you were with me doing the jigsaw as we have done in the past. Reading, editing and advice helped me to see the patterns and find solutions; thanks to Donna, Toni, Caroline, Deb, Tammi, Veronica, Ben, Kaltie, Jocene and Tania.

Finally, to frame and present the jigsaw so that it could be shared with others in an accessible public forum, thanks to Alicia for seeing value and providing the permanent frame through publishing, Natalie and Tess for creative decoration, and Rica for polishing through editing.

About the author

Linda Llewellyn is a non-Indigenous woman who was born in Charters Towers and raised in Brisbane, now residing in Townsville on Bindal and Wulgurukaba lands to be closer to her grandchildren. Linda has been a classroom and behaviour support teacher in the State, Catholic and Independent systems for approximately 30 years. She has had leadership positions in mainstream and Aboriginal and Torres Strait Islander education, particularly at Shalom Christian College in Townsville.

Linda supported pre-service teachers at James Cook University and provided training in Behaviour Support, as well as acting as the Director JCU for the RATEP program (Community-based Aboriginal and Torres Strait Islander Teacher Education Program) in 2007.

As a consultant for Brisbane Catholic Education, Linda has developed policy in student behaviour, conducted training and provided support at the systemic, school, classroom and individual student levels.

Linda was engaged as the PhD scholarship holder for an ARC linkage grant examining effective teaching practices for Indigenous students. She worked part-time at Shalom Christian College as a behaviour support teacher, and for Townsville Catholic Education as a mentor for beginning teachers. She currently consults in behaviour support in schools.

www.ingramcontent.com/pod-product-compliance
Lightning Source LLC
Chambersburg PA
CBHW060230030426
42335CB00014B/1390